A MOTHER'S Way of the Cross

DEBORAH McCANN

XXIII

TWENTY-THIRD PUBLICATIONS

Mystic, Connecticut

Fifth printing 1997

Twenty-Third Publications
185 Willow Street
P.O. Box 180
Mystic, CT 06355
(860) 536-2611
(800) 321-0411

ISBN 0-89622-447-3

Introduction

Where, in the midst of lost socks, skinned knees, over-scheduled days, bedtime tantrums, and missed curfews can a mother find time for the Stations of the Cross? Probably nowhere.

But a mother, by doing the myriad tasks she must do every day, can often feel as if she is dragging a heavy cross along the same road Jesus dragged his cross. She's dealing with the complexities of a newborn, the sometimes dangerous explorations of a toddler, or the frustrating, changing role she experiences with an adolescent, and all the fears that come with that stage of life.

This is a Way of the Cross for mothers, written from a mother's viewpoint. In seeing Jesus' struggle up the road to Calvary, we can see our own hopes, fears, and dreams for our children, our triumphs and failures, our lack of courage, sometimes our lack of hope. Though the examples come from my own experience with a young child, I think that what mothers share is universal, no matter what age our children may be. Whether you are a new mother or your children have long been on their own, I hope these meditations will help you discover and remember how your own life is reflected in every step of Jesus' journey. As we reflect on this, our lenten prayer can help us take our own place, sharpen our focus, remember our baptismal calling, renew our strength, and find our way in him.

Jesus Is Condemned

Jesus faced his accusers and accepted the sentence to die on a cross like a common criminal. Pilate condemned him to death, and Jesus was led off to begin his journey to Calvary.

Reflection

When I first learned I was going to be a mother, all kinds of things happened to me. There were the obvious physical changes and moments of exhilaration and great joy. But there were also times when I wondered about my baby's future and my ability to cope with the changes a baby would cause in my life. I started to wonder what kind of mother I'd be, how good a job I'd do.

In talking with other mothers, I realized that these were universal concerns. We shared our feelings about the many frightening and anxious moments we would face as our children grew, moments like waiting to hear that our newborns are healthy and strong, hearing them cry when they get their first shot, seeing them hurt and bleeding when they come from playing, leaving them with sitters or day-care providers, watching them go off to school and knowing how innocent and vulnerable they still are, worrying about drugs and alcohol and teenage problems and behavior. We began to see that caring about children doesn't stop after pregnancy, doesn't stop after infancy, indeed, doesn't stop *ever*.

Even in the days before we knew our children face to face, we sometimes felt overcome by anxiety and felt "condemned" to a "life sentence."

Prayer

Jesus, you were led to die as you had lived—giving of yourself so that others might have life. Help us to remember that your mother is the greatest of disciples because she also heard and accepted God's word, and willingly gave of herself. Help us to follow her example, and to see our own motherhood as one of the joyful, and sometimes painful, ways that we are called to be your disciples.

Latin Cross

Jesus Carries the Cross

The guards did not let Jesus off easy. Before he had to shoulder the burden of his cross, he was ridiculed, spat upon, whipped, and humiliated. Yet he persevered and picked up and carried the cross.

Reflection

Motherhood teaches us that God's wisdom is enormous, God's love all-encompassing. During the months before a baby is born, God sends great joy. Anxiety and fear are balanced by hope and anticipation as each new day brings new growth. The baby kicks, rolls over, punches and pounds, as a reminder of its presence. As the being inside shows more and more life, joy deepens. After the baby is born, watching it stretch and wave its fists reminds us of movements we felt within. We find that we have come to know and love this child with all of our being, and the cross seems light. Suddenly, in these familiar gestures of our newborn, we realize that we are not alone; this child has been with us and will continue to be with us for a long time.

As time goes on and we glory in our child's headlong embrace of the world, laughing and crying at each new discovery, watching as he or she accepts new brothers and sisters into the family, seeing the great streak of independence that we welcome and yet want to hinder, we realize that the acceptance of a mother's responsibility, though a burden, is a joyful one, and one greeted with happiness.

Prayer

Jesus, your cross was a way of love that led to life and joy. Help us to remember the times of great joy that we share with our children and to see, in our sharing, the path that leads to ever deeper love.

Celtic Cross

Jesus Falls the First Time

Weakened as he was by the beating and the weight of the cross, Jesus fell to the ground. The soldiers roughly dragged him to his feet and pressed him onward.

Reflection

Along with the joy of a child comes an undreamed-of sense of frustration and let-down. Patience is a prized virtue as we struggle to retain our composure in the face of these demanding newborn creatures who are completely dependent on us in a way that nothing has been before. From the early all-nighters and the days of colic, through all the stages of our children's growth, we can feel ready to scream, tied down as never before, trapped with a wailing infant, an imperious toddler, a rebellious teenager, with no end in sight.

Somehow we should have serenity and control. We should feel maternal instinct welling up within us, but the reality is far from the pastel pictures painted of joyful motherhood. As Jesus fell the first time under the enormity of his cross, we can feel that we're falling as well—and failing.

Prayer

Jesus, help us to see the light at the end of the tunnel. Help us to remember that these children of ours are treasured gifts, just as insecure and untested in this world as we are at caring for them. Give us the patience and the courage to persevere, and help us grow together in our life in you.

St. Andrew's Cross

Jesus Meets His Mother

Mary was following Jesus on his road to Calvary. At one point they came face to face. What could she do? What could she say to him? What words of comfort and love could overcome this terrible moment? What did he think of her, now?

Reflection

Sometimes I wonder how our children will see us in years to come. Which will be most remembered, the care and the love, the cuddling and the comforting, or those times when we had to put them aside to get back to work, the times we had to leave them with care providers, the times we responded with impatience or inattention when they needed to talk or be held, or the times they looked to us for help and there was so very little we could do? I can see Jesus looking at Mary and her looking back, and the myriad of messages that must have passed between those eyes.

When young, our children accept us utterly, but as they grow, they begin to see our flaws, and they often seem far more patient than we, far more open to new ideas, and willing to fight for their right to live their own lives, no matter how wrong-headed we might find them. We take comfort that they also receive joy and laughter and undivided attention—during those times we can freely give them. But is it enough? Can they realize that they are the most significant part of our lives, but that there are other parts as well that need just as much attention? Can they accept our limitations? Can *we* accept our limitations?

Prayer

Jesus, help us to do our best to give and love with the entirety of our being. Help us also to remember that we cannot be perfect, and that we, too, must sometimes rely on the acceptance, mercy, and love of others.

St. Peter's Cross

Station Five

Simon Helps Jesus

Simon was a stranger, a foreigner in Jesus' land. He was dragged out of the crowd by the soldiers to help Jesus carry the cross. Like the Good Samaritan, he was a stranger, yet he helped the person in need.

Reflection

I always used to laugh at the "Calgon, take me away!" commercial as being just a lot of advertising hype. I now know that it's untruthful as well—what did that mother *do* with her family while she locked herself away for a soothing, refreshing dip in the tub?! There are many days I long for a Simon to help me with my cross, when my neatly organized list of things to do remains untouched because of constant interruptions. But, in calmer moments, I see how much time my husband spends with our child to give me a chance to put my feet up even for a few minutes, how he'll cook dinner or wash the dishes (oftentimes both) to give me a break. How I treasure the closeness my child has with his grandparents, and how glad I am that we live near enough that they can visit him often.

There are many Simons in each day, if we can only recognize them.

Prayer

Jesus, help us to count our blessings and welcome help, instead of trying to be superwomen who must do everything ourselves or else count ourselves failures. Help us to remember that your presence and support often come through other people. Help us to see you in the warm glances, reassuring hugs, and helping hands offered by the people we meet every day.

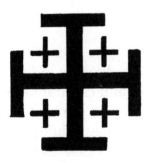

Jerusalem Cross

Veronica Wipes Jesus' Face

We don't know who Veronica was, but tradition says she came forward through the line of guards surrounding Jesus to wipe his face clean of the mud and blood and sweat that covered it. It was a thoughtful, compassionate gesture.

Reflection

It's a terrifying thing to be awakened in the middle of the night by a child's cry of fear. The comforting helps both parent and child. It helps parents to conquer their own fears as they soothe the child. What nameless terrors possess children in their dreams? How can we help to ease those terrors when we can't put a name to them? How much love we feel as we hold and rock our children and feel them relax and drift back to sleep.

During the day, do we respond as quickly and compassionately as Veronica did to Jesus' unspoken need, or are we too wrapped up in our own world to recognize when our children are hurting or fearful or just need a quick hug or reassuring pat? Do we always respond with good grace at bids for attention, or are we short and sharp? Are we always ready to mediate wisely in their quarrels, respecting their sense of self and territory, or do we treat them as insignificant, "childish," or unimportant? Are we wise enough to know when our children really need attention, or are we constantly keeping our eye on something else? Are we as compassionate as we can be?

Prayer

Jesus, help us to comfort wisely and well. Help us to remember that our children look to us for so many things, and need us more than any job or daily task ever could. The days when they'll need us will pass before we know it, and we will miss them. Help us to treasure these days while they're here.

Passion Cross

Jesus Falls Again

Jesus fell a second time as weariness overcame him. But the guards had no sympathy. They pulled him to his feet again and pushed him along.

Reflection

In spite of our great resolve to be constantly aware and nurturing to our children, there are the times when we let our jobs take precedence. There are other times when we have just finished cleaning the house, putting everything in its place, only to turn around and discover that a child has been following right along behind us scattering debris. There are times when all is still, and we can settle down for a little private time of reading or knitting, only to have one of our children wake up bright and alert and ready to play. These are the times when we can really feel boxed in, when all this caring and attention seems unbearably confining.

It's important to remember that we're only human, that shortness of temper and lack of patience are part and parcel of that humanity. We can only strive to be better. In the striving is the reward.

Prayer

Jesus, help us to gain more patience today. Help us to remember that you fell more than once but kept on going, and that love can guide us when the sacrifice seems too great.

Cross Potent

The Women Weep for Jesus

In the crowd that surrounded Jesus was a group of professional mourners who followed along weeping and wailing. Jesus saw them and admonished them to turn to matters that should really concern them rather than doing a lot of false weeping for him.

Reflection

So many times we find ourselves almost overcome when talking with other mothers about childhood development, grades, or achievements, and we are tempted to compare our children with theirs. We feel so inadequate when we skim magazines filled with triumphant stories of "supermoms" who seem to have done it all—the career, the childrearing, the time (and energy!) for tender, candlelit dinners and private time with their spouses. Like the professional mourners who followed Jesus, these stories and people can cause all of us to lose sight of our own universe, to question our ability and skill in all sorts of situations.

Jesus told the women to weep for themselves and their children. Can we turn our attention to our own children, to enjoy and wonder at their growth, to take satisfaction in getting a job done on time with enough time left over to bake cookies and let them play with the dough? It's the small moments of each day that mean the most, the small accomplishments that can reaffirm our faith in ourselves.

Prayer

Jesus, help us to stop focusing on our situation by envying that of others. Help us to remember that *we* are the only persons to compare ourselves with, that small satisfactions can be very great indeed, and that the only thing that really counts in the end is how closely we have followed the path you have set out for us.

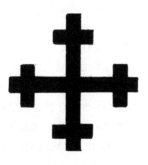

Cross–Crosslet

Jesus Falls the Third Time

Near the end of his journey, as he traveled up the hill to Calvary, Jesus again lost his footing and fell. How hard it must have been for him to get up again and go forward, knowing what awaited him.

Reflection

Those of us who have been blessed with healthy children find the times when they fall ill especially trying. Sick children are impatient to be well and get back to being with their friends, and they grow demanding, waking at night for water, whimpering when fever hurts, needing constant and complete attention from us. These are the times when our patience is at a minimum, when seeking it can be yet another frustration. Knowing our children need us, trying to keep a cheerful and compassionate face, responding immediately and fully to whatever they need, understanding how they hate to be tied down even for a day or two, getting them to sit still for medicines they dislike—these are small but wearing trials.

How hard it must be for mothers whose children are chronically or terminally ill! What constant heartache they must feel. They must start each new day with hopes that may be dashed, and improvements that may be fleeting at best. Our trials are nothing to theirs, a pure exercise in self-pity.

Prayer

Jesus, help us to put our petty annoyances in perspective. Help us to remember that you kept on your journey even after collapsing for the third time. Help us, too, to feel the lightness of our own crosses in comparison with those others must bear, and to do our part to bring your strength and consolation to them, to be part of your loving presence in the world.

St. Anthony's Cross

Jesus Is Stripped

Once at Calvary, Jesus was stripped of his garments and left to stand naked and alone in front of the crowd, his followers and strangers alike. How helpless and foolish he must have looked to those who believed in him, how helpless and foolish he must have felt.

Reflection

When he was only two, my child needed an operation that filled me with fear. His composure was admirable; I was completely undone. My "good face" was full of tear-stained smiles—he was calm and accepting. After it was over, the doctors and nurses were amazed at how well he had done, how cooperative and patient he had been. What does that say of him, and of me?

Again and again, without meaning to, without taking the time to count to ten, we have lashed out at our children, overreacting to simple accidents of childhood, being impatient with our adolescent's know-it-all attitude, placing blame where admonition or understanding would do. In some of these moments, we see them watching us. We see them trying to be the comforter instead of the comforted, accepting our outbursts with love and trust, and in the process, without meaning to, making us feel smaller than ever. It's hard to tell these children who look to us for guidance that we have been wrong. It's hard to accept blame instead of placing it. In those moments, how helpless and foolish we feel.

Prayer

Jesus, help us to accept these moments of nakedness before our children. Help us to remember that in seeing us as we are in times of fear and stress, they can learn that fears, compassion, imperfection, vulnerability, and forgiveness are all part of human life. Help us, too, to always be able to ask forgiveness, especially from these children, when we have been wrong.

Lorraine Cross

Jesus Is Nailed to the Cross

If there was a moment when Jesus realized there was no turning back, it must have been when the nails went through his hands and feet, binding him to the cross. Now there was no escape, no way to avoid death.

Reflection

A toddler busily discovering the world presents far different adventures and challenges than an infant. For the first time, discipline enters the picture, and the word "no" becomes as familiar a part of a child's vocabulary as it does ours. As babyhood gives way to childhood and then to adolescence, our commitment takes on a new face. Suddenly our responsibility goes beyond simple caring and tending and involves the sharing of values and the teaching of right and wrong.

This realization came to me clearly at my child's baptism. When my husband and I stood together proclaiming our faith and initiating our child into our church community, we felt like real parents for the first time. We realized that our mission as parents included helping our child to know and love our God and grow as part of God's people. That mission isn't always an easy one, especially when we are plagued by our own doubts and temptations, or when our children seem more eager to listen to other voices that do not speak of our values. Helping our children be open to the gift of faith is an awesome and difficult challenge.

Prayer

Jesus, when you were nailed to the cross, you knew there was no turning back from your mission. Help us to remember the enormity of our baptismal responsibility. Guide us in teaching our children, giving reasons and love along with the rules, so that we may grow in faith and love together.

St. Julian's Cross

Jesus Dies on the Cross

Alone in spite of the people gathered at his feet, Jesus felt abandoned even by his father in heaven as he breathed his last and died. At that moment his followers surely lost all hope and faith in Jesus and in his mission.

Reflection

There is no question that children change us completely. Our time is no longer our own, and any precious moments we can snatch away for ourselves are to be treasured. There comes a day when we suddenly realize the enormity of this change, how totally these children have transformed the way we respond to everything.

Career goals and life plans we may have made for ourselves very often cannot be met or must be scaled back, and dreams of glory, fame, and achievement are sacrificed for what we hope is a higher good. It can be an enormous struggle, too, not to try and live out our own dreams of glory in our children, but to let them find their own ways.

Just as Jesus died to save us all, we die to self in the name of our children. Jesus' death was an enormous defeat for his followers, and they saw all their hopes dashed. But in that death was the glory of the resurrection to come.

Prayer

Jesus, help us to see that losing some goals opens the door to others. Help us to remember that your ultimate sacrifice of love is repeated daily in how we live our lives and how we share the gifts you have given us with our children. Help us to see the life-affirming reality of your resurrection in our children each day.

Papal Cross

Jesus Is Taken Down from the Cross

Jesus' lifeless body was taken down from the cross. He had died in agony, and only Joseph of Arimathea offered a burial place for him. Mary cradled Jesus in her arms and wept as his body was carried away.

Reflection

I remember taking a long walk with my husband shortly before our child was born. We held hands and nestled together in these last precious moments as a couple, and wondered what our life would be like when we welcomed this new family member we had never seen, and yet had been so close to for so many months. Should we see a movie? Eat out? Take a long drive? There were so many things we wanted to do, yet we just walked and talked about the future. We were already mourning the loss of our couplehood even as we looked with anticipation to what lay ahead.

Jesus died. He didn't save himself from the cross. When his lifeless body was taken down, his followers lost heart. This was the ultimate defeat—he was really and truly dead. What would life be like without him? When I think of how they must have felt at this darkest of moments, I remember that walk, how it was a time of closing one door and waiting to open another.

Prayer

Jesus, help us to treasure moments of contemplation. Help us to remember that there was no need to despair—the fulfillment of your mission was yet to come, just as we waited and wondered what our new life would bring, just as we still wait and wonder with each passing day.

Greek Cross

Jesus Is Placed in the Tomb

Jesus was wrapped in a shroud, and placed hurriedly in the tomb provided by Joseph. The soldiers and guards rolled an enormous boulder in front of the entrance to make sure that nothing happened to the body—that Jesus' followers couldn't come and steal his body and make more miraculous claims about him.

Reflection

By now, our children are such an integral part of our lives that we can barely remember what life was like without them. Sometimes when spouses are alone all they can talk about is their children— their wonder and enthusiasm and joy as they grasp their world head-on. Our children are their own persons, full of definite opinions (and not at all wary of sharing them!). We want to laugh when they laugh and weep when they weep. We share their anxiety when their concerns seem overwhelming, and we remember how we felt when we were young. Our lives are so different with them, and so much more complete.

When Jesus lay in the tomb, his followers had a chance to take stock and plan for their new life. He gave them a chance to discover their new identity as disciples, before gifting them with his glorious resurrection. We share in this as we see our children grow and change, develop skills, and display talents that may have been hidden for generations. In the lives of our children, we see our lives continued. We may hear and laugh at our parents' voices in our own. And we thank God when our dark moments of despair and frustration are dispelled as we see the resurrection each and every day in our children's eyes.

Prayer

Jesus, thank you for the chance to see your promise of life in the life of our children. Help us to remember what a precious and unique gift these children are, and let our love and care always be reflective of your love for us all.

Anchor Cross

Resurrection

Where, in the midst of lost socks, skinned knees, over-scheduled days, bedtime tantrums, and missed curfews can a mother find time for the Stations of the Cross? Probably nowhere!

But in each of these daily occurrences, the light of the Resurrection shines—the knowledge that everything we do as mothers, everything we go through, is all part of trying to do our best to nurture and support the lives of the children God gives us. The Resurrection is in the faces of each of them, and in the faces of everyone around us who reminds us that we are not alone on our journey.

Jesus' final journey to death and then to glorious new life is our journey, too. Even in our darkest moments, the hope of the Resurrection is shining, if we can find it, if we can remember to seek it.

The triumph of Easter is our triumph, too. Each day is a new beginning for us; each day brings with it the seeds of new hope and joy. Our journey with Jesus does not end with his death—like him, we have the chance for new life, always supported and guided by his love.

Maltese Cross

'Inspirational! Essential reading for anyone wanting to follow a life of Magic and spiritual empowerment.'

ATHENA STARWOMAN ~ MYSTICAL VISIONARY AND AUTHOR

'Here at last is a user-friendly guide to practical witchcraft. Deborah Gray shows us how to gain self-empowerment by opening ourselves to the secret powers of Nature and the Goddess.'

NEVILL DRURY ~ AUTHOR

DEBORAH GRAY

how to
be a
real

Witch

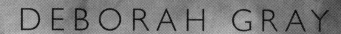
HarperCollinsPublishers

While the author has researched the recipes and spells in this book, ingredients can vary, especially the active ingredients of herbs. Conditions under which the recipes are made may differ, or the products might be used in ways the author could not have anticipated. The author and publishers cannot accept responsibility for any adverse health effects or undiscovered hazards of foods or herbs or essential oils, or for any injuries, losses or other damages that may result from the use of the information in this book.

A note on essential oils:

Some essential oils can be harmful. Please take note of the following points: never apply essential oils directly on your skin; never take essential oils internally; discontinue the use of essential oils immediately if you suffer an allergic reaction, and seek professional advice; never dilute more than a total of eight drops of essential oils in water for vaporisation, unless advised otherwise by a qualified aromatherapist or naturopath; if you are pregnant (or there is a chance you are pregnant) consult a qualified aromatherapist, naturopath, or your family doctor, before using any essential oil; keep oils out of reach of children.

HarperCollins*Publishers*

First published in Australia in 2001
by HarperCollins*Publishers* Pty Limited
ABN 36 009 913 517
A member of the HarperCollins*Publishers* (Australia) Pty Limited Group
http://www.harpercollins.com.au

HarperCollins*Publishers*

25 Ryde Road, Pymble, Sydney, NSW 2073, Australia
31 View Road, Glenfield, Auckland 10, New Zealand
77-85 Fulham Palace Road, London W6 8JB, United Kingdom
Hazelton Lanes, 55 Avenue Road, Suite 2900, Toronto, Ontario M5R 3L2
and 1995 Markham Road, Scarborough, Ontario M1B 5M8, Canada
10 East 53rd Street, New York NY 10022, USA

National Library of Australia Cataloguing-in-Publication data:

Gray, Deborah (Deborah Noëlle)
How to be a real witch.
ISBN 0 7322 6841 9.
1. Deborah Gray (Deborah Noëlle). 2. Witchcraft. 3.
Witches – Australia – Biography. I. Title.
133.43

Cover photograph: Stephen Oxenbury, 2C Management
Cover design: Katie Mitchell, HarperCollins Design Studio
Internal layout: Domenika Markovtzev, Brevier Design
Set in 12/16 Giovanni Book
Printed in Australia by Griffin Press on 79gsm Bulky Paperback White

5 4 3 2 1   01 02 03 04

Dedication

My deepest thanks,

To my mother, for being my living example of the Goddess of
nurturing and unconditional love.

To my father, for showing me the importance of an
independent and searching spirit.

To my grandmother Ruth, for still astonishing us all with such
strength, wisdom and the sparkle of irrepressible youth.

To Giancarlo, my soul mate and partner, for your
never-ending support, love and mystical insight.

To my coven sister Leonora and my star companion and dear friend Athena
— thank you for your eternal support and for helping
keep the Magical flame alive.

And to all the 'goddesses' of HarperCollins, especially Helen Littleton,
Katie Mitchell and Kate Pollard, for all your patience and creativity.

And to all my past, present and future readers,
thank you for helping to make this book possible.

'The brightest of blessings and love to you all!'

contents

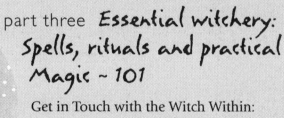

Foreword

WELCOME, FELLOW SEEKER

You may have just started studying witchcraft and Magic, and may be looking around at all the different ways and traditions. Or perhaps you have been studying for a long time and already feel a strong connection to one particular witchy tradition or ancient path. Maybe you just want to enjoy reading about some of the old Magic arts, to add some valuable new insights to your own spiritual knowledge.

Whatever awakened your spirit and set you on your path as a seeker, and whatever brought you here to read this book, or first inspired your journey into Magic is correct and perfect for you.

Every one of us who feels the urge to remember the ancient philosophies and ways of the Wise Ones — whether or not we have been studying for a few months or years as a solitary practitioner, or have lived in a well-established and traditional coven for two or three decades, or have just started reading a few books on the subject — has the right to practise Magic and to say out loud: 'I am a witch'. And that right begins the split second our interest is sparked.

The very moment you awaken your search for Magical knowledge is the moment you consciously become a magician. That may happen when you are inspired by some great words in a book or when you look up at

the sky one night, see the twinkling stars and suddenly realise with wonderful certainty and lucidity that

'Life itself is Magic'.

Many other wonderful and inspiring events can spark that conscious awakening, and it can happen at any age or stage of life.

And from that moment on, if you keep your spiritual goals in focus and keep listening to your inner voice and instincts, if you keep your mind and heart open to learning as much as you can about the mysteries and wonders of the Universe, you will be well on your way to a deeper understanding and eventually the essential practice of the beautiful and inspirational Craft of the Wise.

If you have taken the time to open your heart and mind to self-knowledge, you have already opened the first and most important of many doors — and you have already begun your wonderful journey to becoming a Real Witch.

So congratulations, fellow seeker, and welcome to the world of Magic.

The first part of this book relates to the inner lore and deeper meanings of witchcraft — what being a witch is all about. The second provides essential knowledge and secret keys to get you started as a witch, with 'How to' instructions for spellcasting, and different tools and techniques for Magical mastery and enchantment. The third part is brimming with spells, charms and Magical cures of all kinds for you to enjoy. Any spells mentioned in the other parts of the book are given in detail in this section. The last part is about my own life as a witch — all about my early years as a Sorcerer's apprentice, living in one of Australia's original and most famous covens — followed by an index of the spells, charms and Magical cures.

Introduction

TWILIGHT OF THE SORCERERS

During my early teen years, when I was a young witchling, taking my first steps out into the big wide world, fate jolted me onto an amazing roller coaster ride of life experiences. Along with them came a series of prophetic visions and deep inner reflection. I then set out on a quest to find a spiritual teacher, a Merlin of Magic, who could help reawaken my heritage in the Craft and show me the true ways of the Wise.

And, for whatever reason, the God/dess must have heard me calling, because before long I became a Master's Apprentice to an Old Sorcerer, an adept philosopher of the Occult who in this life and dimension had chosen to teach in the manner of a Druid Master of Witchcraft. An exceptional being who came to feature prominently in my life as a witch.

Now, after 25 years of metaphysical study and a great response to my first spellbooks, I feel the time is here to share the secrets of my own journey into witchcraft, and to reveal more of the deeper insights and mysteries behind this timeless heritage of universal knowledge and enchantment.

I have also been inspired by the sense of a special time approaching. A door of opportunity is reopening and many of us who have journeyed into the Craft and all the other Magical paths are remembering our

xi

Dreamtime Circle. We are coming back together again and all the different old souls are feeling the sense of Gathering; in the Craft we call it the 'Quickening'. You are probably feeling it yourself.

It is a sense of an imminent Golden Age where all of us, whatever our spiritual choices, will have an incredible opportunity for clear vision, to see what's ahead and be able to take definite steps to get there. It's a Magical vision that has been seen and felt before in times past, and is now being awakened within the many different spiritual tribes, including all the indigenous and pagan peoples around this planet. We are experiencing an intensification of enchanted energy, catching glimpses through the mists of time and seeing the magnificent vision of our own potential.

At this special time I have chosen to share my personal journey into witchcraft, which is a unique one, as are all spiritual journeys. Just as I found my way, you too are capable of being a great magician, sorcerer and wizard. The Magic is there inside you, just waiting to be discovered. You have the power to make it real.

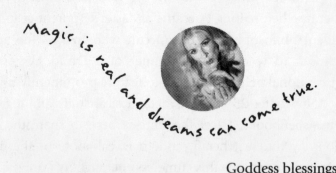

Magic is real and dreams can come true.

Goddess blessings
Deborah Gray

Congratulations, fellow seekers, and welcome to the world of magic...

witch is the way?

What's being a witch all about? ~ Finding your witchy way ~ What's Wicca? ~ Finding a teacher or coven ~ Some inside info (on Magic, manipulation, rules and redes) demons and ghoulies) ~ You hexy witch ~ Your ancient heritage ~ Making natural connections ~ Get into a good head space ~ Witchy wild and free

part one

what's being a witch all about?

first of all, it's a unique experience. Every witch is a magically unique person and will experience their spiritual journey into Magic in their own special way and time.

I've believed in magic since the age of four, when I began casting spells for the nature spirits in my grandmother's garden. By the time I turned 18, I had managed to charm two Prime Ministers and became a Sorcerer's Apprentice. And while I enjoyed a successful life in public as a TV actress and singer, I was also being privately educated in the ancient mysteries and living in one of the world's best schools of wizardry and witchcraft.

I've studied and practised the Craft for over 25 years, and now as a grown-up witchy woman and artist, I'm still on a wonder-filled and magical quest as I travel the world performing, writing and lecturing about it.

Every witch comes to the Craft in different ways and sees Magic through different eyes and cultures. But witches all over the world, in the past, present and future seem to have a shared spirit and motivation—and that is the quest for truth and knowledge.

Witches and alchemists have always known that great magical power comes to those who know how to tap into the eternal Life Force and the

wisest of them also knew that the greatest power comes with attaining self- knowledge and harmony. A real witch lives a life filled with free-spirited creativity, a passionate sense of the mystical world and a boundless love for Earth and Nature. This is a Craft that is about exploring the ways of the Universe and connecting you with the infinite source of ancient wisdom and alchemy, it's about becoming a Magical Master of your own life, empowered with your own and the eternal energies of all that is, and all that has ever been.

Oh, yes and it's also about casting spells—with all of the above in mind. And what all we witches have common access to—those already practising and all the wannabe witches-in-waiting—

is the source of real Magic

Once you get the hang of it, and you've connected to the source of Real Magic, it becomes a part of you and a life asset that you always have with you. Whatever path into the Craft you may choose, inside and out, you're a mobile Magicmaker, ready to switch on, plug into the eternal Life Force and weave your spells and charms wherever and whenever you want to.

Living with Magic is an integral part of what I do and feel every day. One of my favourite sayings is: 'If you don't believe in Magic, how can Magic believe in you?' After all, if you don't believe in yourself, how can other people believe in you? I think that it's so important for people to realise that they are spiritual and magical beings. And for me, that knowledge is one of the most powerful tools in my life. Of course, everyone is different and not everyone has the time or the inclination to learn all the techniques or study on the level that a longtime witch, shaman or even an astrologer does. But it is important that whenever something magical happens to you, something that you just know is more than a mere coincidence, that you allow your spirit to acknowledge it. Let yourself stop and feel the

inspiration of that moment, where you can really say to yourself: 'Yes, that was miraculous—that was magic!'

In the study of witchcraft and metaphysics we often look back to days past and the wonderful wisdom of the ancient teachers and philosophies. But I consider that witchcraft is also a living and constantly evolving Craft, and throughout my life I have met modern-day philosophers, masters of metaphysics and 'living goddesses' who practise their own magical and spiritual paths in today's world and are great examples of just how possible it is to successfully apply Magic and spirituality to our modern urban lives on a daily basis. Our lives are full of enchanted and miraculous moments, especially when we take the time to look around and really notice.

As my 'stargoddess' friend Athena often says:

'Don't just wait around for your birthday to make a wish.

Why not do it every day?'

Because every day is a brand-new day of your life, with new challenges and new opportunities. I know from personal experience that once you learn to tap into the eternal Universe and your own inner power, it can really change your life.

Finding Your Witchy Way

Throughout history, there has never been just one 'correct' or 'absolute' way of being a witch or a magician. And neither should there be. Instead, there has always been as many different views and paths as there are people seeking them.

There are many different opinions and cultures in the world, just as there are many different traditions and paths of witchcraft. But it still delights and amazes me, whenever I travel around this planet and speak with the magical elders and high masters of the many different traditions and styles of witchcraft, that many of them share my belief: just like the different tribes of the human race, Magic all comes from the same infinite and loving source and, at its most profound level, the inner core of all magical traditions are actually not very different after all.

Whatever path into the Craft you choose to follow is correct for you because at its highest level, the Craft should always be a path of self-acceptance and freedom of spirit.

Beginners and experienced magicians alike, whatever age or level of practice, are all constantly feeling the Magic in their own way in a free exchange of these ancient ideas and a mutual love of the Earth and Nature.

Magic is a growing, living, metaphysical Craft, and the ways of Witchcraft are diverse, with many different styles and spiritual paths.

Witches of the new millennium enjoy a wide range of magical styles and spiritual choices that include Druidry, Wicca, Voodoo, Faery, Asatru, Celtic, Teutonic, Eclectic, Hedgewitch, Hermetic, Strega, Egyptian Tradition, Pow Wow and Dianic, among many more.

Witchcraft as it is practised today has come from a variety of old and ancient cultures that include Celtic, Anglo-Saxon, Nordic, Roman and Greek paganism, Hebrew, Ancient Egyptian, Asian, Native American and African. There is also a burgeoning interest in Australian Aboriginal Dreamtime traditions. And many of these paths are being woven into a dazzling tapestry of old and new practices, each of them as valid and worthy of tolerance and respect as the others.

What's Wicca?

To gain a better insight into the ways of the Craft, it is helpful to understand the different uses of the Anglo-Saxon word 'Wicca' and how that term is applied to today's fast-growing Wiccan religious/spiritual path. Basically, any witch can rightfully use the ancient term 'Wicca' if they so choose, because the word simply means 'witch' in Old English terminology (some scholars also connect the word 'Wicca' even further back in history, to the Neolithic Indo-European migration and root languages, and it can also mean 'bend' or 'wise one'). However, using the term doesn't automatically mean that a person is an initiate or follower of today's Wiccan traditions or religious practices.

Even within the popular and widespread Wiccan culture, which has done much to awaken and spread positive images of witchcraft and has flourished throughout America, Australia and parts of Europe, there are also many different denominations and eclectic branches. These have grown out of the core traditions set down by the learned and influential Englishman Gerald Gardner in the 1940s and '50s, and redeveloped in the 1960s, '70s and '80s by other famous trailblazers and writers of Wiccan practices such as Alex and Maxine Sanders, Doreen Valiente, Raymond Buckland, Scott Cunningham, Silveravenwolf, Starhawk, and Janet and Stewart Farrar.

My Witchy Way

I practise the Craft as a life path to self-knowledge and spiritual empowerment. I consider my witchy 'way' to not only be from an 'old religion', but actually from the spiritual essence—a 'high psychology' and an inner lore of a very ancient form of universal witchcraft that also flows through the core of both old European 'Wicca' craft and Druidic thought. This 'way' is still practised today by certain Orders of magical adepts and to get to a level of mastery, one needs to work without any dogma or superstitions of any kind.

For instance, my magical teacher used the term 'spiritual master' or 'Druid Master of Witchcraft' in the sense of a 'maestro' of this style of practice. Because he was a spiritual and Occult adept, he was able to pass on knowledge to others, but he was very careful to point out to all his students that he didn't consider himself a leader of a religious cult or a teacher of any one 'belief system' because as he always said to us: 'What you are learning are ancient Occult techniques, a free spirited philosophy and a way into the search for Meaning and Truth—the mastery of which is beyond just one fixed religion or doctrine.'

So which path into Witchcraft is the right one?

I'm a firm believer that 'All roads lead to Rome'...

The road you decide to travel should always be your own choice—it's an important evolution in your personal destiny, after all.

Solitary Practice

Many witches are not initiated into any particular coven tradition, and are not necessarily a part of any defined group or religion. They may prefer instead to study and work their Magic alone, blending the different rituals and various traditions and defining their own spiritual path in their own way.

Such witches are commonly known as 'solitary practitioners', and they may practise alone simply because it is not always practical or desirable to join an established coven or to find a larger study group to meet with on a regular basis. 'Hedgewitch' is another term for a 'solitary practitioner' and can be traced back to the old German word 'hagarvassa', meaning 'one who rides on the hedge and boundaries'. This symbolises the person who guards the barriers between the material and the spiritual world, as well as the old folk tradition of the village witch who usually lived alone, in the last cottage on the edge or 'hedge' of town.

In fact, solitary practice is an old-established tradition in itself with a long history in Europe and the British Isles.

Most solitary practitioners of the past were natural adepts who worked alone as village herbalists, healers and folk charmers. The well-documented 'kenning' or 'cunning' men and women are a perfect example of this old tradition. Some were born into a hereditary line of closeknit family groups who quietly passed down their folk traditions to a next of kin.

8

The Coven Concept

Except perhaps for the ancient Druid Magical study groups way back in the pre-Christian era, and some well-hidden secret societies during 'post pagan' times, in Europe and the British Isles it was in fact quite rare to find groups of witches being able to live together or regularly study together in one place. This was particularly true during the tumultuous years of religious superstition that existed from the 11th to the 18th century, and remained relatively the same until the 20th century, when anti-witchcraft laws slowly started being repealed in different countries around the world.

Actual (as opposed to superstitious fantasy stories) 'witch festivals' and full coven gatherings in the woods or outdoors were also uncommon throughout the last thousand years or so. Understandably so, considering the incredible difficulties it would have involved to safely organise meetings during times when witchcraft and any type of magical practice or alternative spirituality were misunderstood and thoroughly persecuted.

Nowadays we are living in a much more tolerant era and, thanks to a loosening up of philosophical and spiritual rights and a growing public awareness, witches of all kinds can gather together or practise alone and unhindered in more and more countries around the world.

The Craft in all its forms is finally becoming much more accepted and understood for the spiritually empowering and Nature-loving path it was originally meant to be.

Finding a Teacher or Coven

Witchcraft is a working craft where you are learning to understand and work with both the known physical world and the spiritual metaphysical world. And there are different types of teachers and schools.

Firstly, there are the 'tools and technology' teachers who usually run workshops that teach 'witch friendly' material such as crystals, astrology, tarot and palm reading, aromatherapy and herbalism. These kinds of teachers and public courses are easily found by looking in the advertising section of New Age and witchcraft magazines, or by going along to the various 'mind, body, spirit' festivals that are always being held at different times and cities throughout the country. Alternatively there are lots of good teaching books available for either beginners or advanced students that go into detail about these kinds of witchy tools and technologies.

Secondly, there are the spiritual teachers and the occult masters of witchcraft. These are either solitary mentors or coven leaders, and the good ones are genuine elders who are highly respected and have developed their mastery over many years (a true elder is someone with at least 15 or 20 years of experience). They are much more private and are rarely found simply by looking in the Yellow Pages.

Finding the right teacher or coven is a very personal thing.

The fact that you have to do your own research, and strive to follow your own way and instincts to find them, is an important and ancient part of the Craft process.

I've had quite a few important magical guides and mentors in my life, the very first and by no means least being my own mother and father—

both of them intuitive philosophers of life who first set me on my witchy way by showing me the importance of self knowledge and a searching spirit. They raised me with a great sense of natural wonder and respect for all things Magical and mystical.

But coming face to face with 'my Merlin' was a major turning point in my life, a truly bewitching moment. My first meeting with Fenris—the Master Druid—was one of recognition and certainty that I was Home, where I belonged, and in the presence of a master of metaphysical knowledge and the ways of ancient mysteries and witchcraft.

While still a teenager, I had started looking further into the inner lore of witchcraft and took my first conscious step to finding a spiritual mentor by actually focusing on that very thought and putting it out into the Universe. As well as going deeper into my own Celtic heritage, I began a complete frenzy of mystical awakening as I studied astrology, the tarot and the power of crystals, practised throwing the I Ching, and looking into yoga, meditation and the spiritual teachings of the Eastern philosophies, including Buddhism and Hinduism. It took a lot of searching and time, but when I was ready, it seemed

the Universe was ready to provide

my next important teacher and mentor of Magic.

In your own search for your witchy way, you may also want to send a thought message out to the universe for a guide or magical mentor like I did. Or you may want to find more of a study group and learn from a few different teachers. You could take witchy workshops, or get together with a circle of friends and compare magical notes and techniques. Or if the opportunity arises, you may want to join a coven.

During the 1970s I not only joined, but also lived in a close family-like environment inside a coven house (coven-bound, some people call it). This unusual way of life doesn't suit everyone, but for me it was a wonderful spiritual foundation stone that has guided me well throughout my careers and my entire adult life, thanks to a spiritual master who was connected to an ancient way of the Craft and lovingly advised me, and our inner circle, of a true and wonderful sense of magical wisdom and alchemy. Edgar (Fenris, the Druid Master) not only taught the ancient mysteries and magic, but he also focused on ways to bring balance and harmony to our everyday lives in and out of the coven. If we ever had a coven motto, it would have been:

'Walk the middle way and keep a sense of balance'.

He taught me not to overdo anything or let the Magic ceremonies and spellcasting overshadow the work I needed to do every day on my inner self.

It was a typical, old Druidic style apprenticeship, which consists of step-by-step, one-on-one training over many years and also included the study of Magic and Occult lore, parapsychology, and the use of logic, music and poetry.

We didn't learn the Craft from a Wiccan style 'book of shadows', which was originated by the English witch Gerald Gardner, when he created the first Wiccan workbook and coven diary in the 1940s. Actually, old 'folk' traditions and earlier witches didn't keep those type of written records, as they mainly passed on the knowledge orally through the generations. But now, with a new found tolerance and the freedom to 'come out' in the open, this contemporary method of teaching and writing down the

Real Magic is taught in the spirit of love and support. Real Magic is learnt in the spirit of love and support. Real Magic is stronger in the spirit of love and support.

important rituals and spells is practised not only by Wiccan practitioners, but also many other styles of witches. It has become an integral part of modern witchcraft.

My early training was from the 'mouth to ear' oral tradition of the Craft, and an emphasis on the mind/body/spirit connection, so my secret grimoire handed down through the generations is called 'the whispering book'. Edgar preferred that we commit most things to memory, which is an important part of the 'Bardic' style technique and is a great skill to learn. But as the years went on, I also started writing down much of the coven training into my own beautifully engraved spellbook, which I like to call the 'book of secrets', and some of it I've included in this book. I decided it was time to start writing down as much as I could, to make sure this information wasn't lost and could be passed on to future generations of covens and solitary witches. By the way, apart from the name 'book of shadows' or the 'book of secrets', some other witches like to call their personal diary 'the wishing book' or their 'magical grimoire'.

A Good Approach

If you choose to find a mystical teacher or coven, keep in mind that the most profound and valuable thing that even the greatest of Grand Masters and spiritual teachers can do is to help guide you to your own inner Magic and knowledge.

When you first start looking for a study group or teacher, one of the most important things to remember is not to rush it. Don't let yourself be pushed into anything or feel rushed by anyone else, and that applies to all aspects of student/teacher and human relationships. Take your time.

Do your own research into what information and teachers are available, and also have a good think about whether or not you are ready for a teacher or really need one. After all, you may very well prefer to remain a solitary practitioner and *experience your Magical journey in your own way and in your own time.*

And that would be absolutely your choice and a perfect decision.

You don't have to find a teacher or be initiated into any type of coven to be a genuine witch, because all the eternal knowledge and wisdom of the universe is already there inside you and may be awakened in different ways.

For instance, many people are naturally gifted and some may have 'crossed the abyss' through extraordinary experiences and life-changing events that are in a real sense the ultimate kind of initiation into true knowledge.

Read any books that appeal to you, and that you understand and feel comfortable with. Most importantly, follow your gut instincts about people, spiritual mentors, schools, study groups, teachers, Websites and covens.

You know that funny feeling in the pit of your stomach? Well those tummy butterflies are wise little creatures and will never steer you wrong. When they start fluttering, sit quietly and listen.

Is This the Right Teacher or Coven?

If you do come across a potential mentor or coven, step back and observe how the mentor or coven leader is applying Magic to their own lives before you entrust them with guiding yours.

Most covens have some type of leader, hierarchical system or high priestess/priest, and their magical purpose and direction is usually steered by the leader or leaders.

Don't be overly impressed by lofty titles alone or certificates that say 'graduate of Occult studies' or 'initiated by such and such into such and such Craft lineage'. The growing popularity of this type of certificate is a new phenomenon in the Craft and I wouldn't recommend using them alone to judge someone's expertise as a spiritual guide.

Instead, ask yourself this series of simple and logical questions, then listen to what your inner gut voice tells you:

- ◉ Do their teachings appear to be working for them?

- ◉ Does the teacher or coven leader appear to follow their own spiritual advice and apply their knowledge and techniques successfully into their own normal everyday lives?

- ◉ How many years have they been doing this?

- ◉ Do they seem to cope pretty well with the normal ups and downs of daily life?

- ◉ How does this person act when they are with you and with other people? Do they respect your decisions, personal freedom, independence and right to make your own choices?

- ◉ All teachers need to be confident and strong-willed, and may even have to be quite assertive with disruptive or noisy students. But does this person generally appear kind, tolerant and patient with you and others?

- During your magical lessons, does the coven leader or teacher answer questions well, and can they converse naturally and spontaneously about their own specialty and path? Or, if they are a more eclectic teacher, can they speak easily about their own valuable experiences, visionary ideas and different Magical subjects?

- And, most importantly for a spiritual teacher or coven leader, do they show a well-balanced and mature perspective on life, and are they loved and respected by their students and friends?

Let's face it, there is no point in joining a circle, coven or study group where the head of the group is immature or inexperienced, or can't cope with the responsibility, or if they're someone who is unstable, or stuck in a distorted view of witchcraft.

If you are confident that the spiritual mentor or high priest or priestess is both highly respected and experienced, feel free to ask them lots of questions before you join their circle, group or coven.

They should respect and understand your natural interest and concerns.

Some Inside Info

Before we go any further, here's some inside information, straight from the witch's mouth, to dispel some myths that surround the subject of Magic. Firstly, are Magic spells manipulative? What's the chance of calling up a demon? When does a witch use her hexing powers? And, finally, can a man be a witch, and if so, what do we call him?

Magic or Manipulation?

Witches have been casting love spells, making healing medicines and good-luck charms, doing astrology charts and looking into the past and future for thousands of years. We spend our whole life looking at the hidden, Occult mysteries and how the science and Magic of the universe works, and that includes bending time and space and inventing ways to cause changes within ourselves and the world around us.

If someone wants to classify that as manipulation, they would be at least half right. But that is the essence of witchcraft and alchemy. This is, after all, the Craft of 'bending and weaving'.

But it's our own universe we are 'bending and weaving', and we study Magic and cast our spells to help us become masters of our own lives.

For hundreds of years, there has been a myth and distorted perception that witches take over another person's 'free will' when casting a love spell or that they control other people with their Magic. That is one of the main reasons witches were persecuted in the past, and it is really a lot of superstitious nonsense left over from the Dark Ages.

A Magic spell performed correctly can certainly change the atmosphere and greatly alter the dynamic flow—the energy patterns—between two or more people, which in itself is an incredible feat.

A powerful sorcerer can 'bend' and 'weave' perceptions and dynamic

energies, which in turn may have an effect on the choice another person is going to make. But that person's final decision and ultimate choice is always made according to their own free will and universal destiny, and that can't be taken away by or replaced with a spell.

Now this is where logic comes into play when working with Magic, and if you are really interested in the inner lore and High Magic of the craft, the following information is important to think about.

Our god/dess Nature endows us all with the gift of free will so that we have the ultimate choice and responsibility for our own lives. Your free will is yours alone and is one of your greatest powers. It gives you the ability to shape your own life and future.

No-one else has the power to take that away from you—and you don't have the power to take it away from anyone else—not with a Magic spell or any other enchantment.

This is one of those natural laws of the universe that many people (including some witches) either misunderstand or are too caught up in superstitious beliefs to think about clearly.

Magic can't completely go outside the Laws of the Universe; it doesn't work that way, and that's not the point of the exercise.

The influence a witch has on others is fleeting, but the influence they have on themselves and their own destiny is huge, and that is what a Real Witch looks for and where their greatest Magical power lies.

There are thousands of people in the world who now follow the pagan or goddess way of spiritual worship and devote their life to it as their path or religion, and there are many people among them who don't call themselves witches or cast any spells, which is completely their right and choice.

Not all pagans practise Magic and Witchcraft. And not all witches follow a pagan religion.

If someone follows certain elements of magic and the Craft but at the same time feels it is wrong or strictly against their beliefs to go ahead and use their acquired skills, then I also wouldn't call them a 'witch'.

Weaving charms and casting spells is certainly a part of what witches did in the past, what they've finally got the freedom to do again, and—with a dash of luck—what we will still be doing for many millennia to come.

'Take hold of your own lives. Most of the things that distress you, you can avoid, and most of the things that dominate you, you can overthrow. You can do what you will with them.'

Plato, 400 BC

Rules and Redes

There are a lot of different opinions around about what is 'good' and what is 'bad' or manipulative Magic. People also speak often about the 'laws of threefold return'.

Quite a few paths within the Craft have their own rules and what they call 'redes'. These are more like guides or suggestions for 'higher-minded' behaviour, and are not absolute laws of witchcraft.

Contrary to popular belief, the current forms of written redes are not from ancient religious texts and so-called 'witches' laws', or from any known ancient practice of the Craft. They are primarily a 20th-century creation.

The widely known 'Wiccan Rede' was first set down by the influential Gerald Gardner for his own book of shadows, and as a guide to his more publicly accessible magical practices around the 1940s. Since then, it has been adapted and revised many times by the leaders and spiritual writers of the different Wiccan and neo-goddess traditions that came after.

You will often see the phrases 'an it harm none, do as thou will' and 'the Law of threefold return' written into many modern books on witchcraft and Wicca. These popular phrases weren't actually derived from old writings of Celtic or British Wicca Craft; they are symbolic terms that have been adapted from a variety of different sources and cultures, including the Freemasons and Rosicrucians, Alistair Crowley and some of the Asian-based 'karmic' philosophies such as Buddhism.

Both of these terms are lovely analogies which suggest that whatever energy you send out will eventually be returned to you, and if you allow the 'intent' of your actions to be for a positive transformation, you will receive a positive outcome.

Whatever rules and redes a modern witch may choose to work under, he or she is still surrounded by the inevitable Laws of Nature.

That doesn't apply only to Magic. Every action you take in life causes not just one or threefold reactions but a myriad of effects. It's always wise to think anything through and 'look before you leap'.

Man-made rules and religious guidelines depend on individual choices and beliefs. But if you are concerned about 'karma' and would like to feel confident you are following a 'higher minded' Magic, follow these steps: try and maintain a fair-minded and well-balanced outlook during your normal everyday life; spend time looking into your inner self and keep working to gain spiritual and emotional awareness and harmony; then the judgment you always know you can trust is your own.

Always remember that it's best to follow your own true will and judgment when casting your spells and charms, because that's where most of your power comes from.

22

Demons and Ghoulies

Don't worry, modern witchcraft is not about trying to raise up nasty demons and ghoulies. And even if you wanted to waste your time trying, you'd have more chance of flying to Mars on a broomstick than raising even a slightly cranky dust mite.

This kind of legend and bad press in witchcraft is left over from the days of religious persecution, when anyone who was even remotely an alternative thinker was labelled a heretic and thought to be invoking demons and evil spirits.

The Hollywood-style witchcraft that you see in films and teen TV shows—with all of the invoking of entities and calling up well-dressed demons (à la *Charmed*)—is great fun and very entertaining, but it's all just fantasy, the product of a scriptwriter's vivid imagination.

Throughout the many years I've spent as a witch, and been practising Magic both alone and with different Occult masters, I've found nothing to fear in the supernatural or Occult world.

Yes, of course there are many fascinating and awe-inspiring energies swirling around the metaphysical plane.

23

But that is also true of the 'real' physical world we live in every day and night; it too is packed full of incredible and mysterious energy. (If you've ever been to the post-Christmas sales, you'll know just what I mean.)

Everyone on the planet, not just witches, manages to live side by side and quite comfortably with a whole array of incredible energies and powers on a daily basis. In fact, most people don't think twice about it. Next time you see the sun peeking through the clouds, catch a glimpse of the ocean or watch a bolt of lightning flash in a thunderstorm, just think about how much amazing power and energy there is right here in our 'normal' lives. No wonder the Ancients gave these natural phenomena names like Thor the god of Thunder, Amon Ra the Sun god and Neptune the Lord of the Sea.

You see, what many people may think of as 'supernatural' or 'from the otherworld' is just another dimension of the whole picture of Nature and ourselves.

So try and abandon any superstitions or fears from spellcasting and rituals. The study of Magic will allow you to open up to all the possibilities of the universe, and to encourage your own human and spiritual development.

The natural universe has its own in-built protective system—an uncanny awareness of the level of your understanding and what you can and can't cope with.

Trust in it.

24

Your intent is like a guiding light ~ a supplier that carries your Magic to its purpose.

You Hexy Witch

Our Universe is alive with a constant ebb and flow of 'yin and yang', or 'positive and negative' energies.

There's no doubt about it—a master magician who has studied the Laws of Nature knows how to both heal and hex and they follow their own instincts in whatever their choice of magical action.

Just as there are great benefits for all of us in the ever-changing seasons—the flow between night and day, summer and winter—there are also great benefits to be gained from embracing both your light-hearted and 'bright goddess' nature, as well as loving your strong, assertive and 'dark goddess' nature.

But there is no point in embracing all that you are and never using it to help yourself or others.

A Real Witch knows that Nature is All that Is

It's a bit silly to think that the universe puts your magic or anything else you do into just 'positive' or 'negative' categories. That is exactly what your own free will and instincts are for—to give you the choice and ability to make your own judgments.

Recently, I've seen a lot of websites and read many books on the Craft that happily talk all about our luscious and witchy 'dark goddess' nature, but then the material falls short on explaining how or when to use it, or curiously advises that it's not 'good' to use these powers for spellworking. On the other hand, many people may read about the 'neutral' path of a real witch and get confused when they are told that there is no such thing as a 'white witch'.

Firstly, let me clear up some of the confusion about the term 'white' or 'good witch'. There is a long, illustrious history of respected Craft healers,

who liked to call themselves 'white witches' after the ancient 'White Goddess' or 'White Lady Moon', and often because they wanted the public and any 'outsiders' to clearly understand the *intent* of their magic. But of course, those magicians knew about the balance of nature and they also had the ability to hex. They understood all aspects of their power to help others and themselves whenever it was needed, and this thriving old 'white' healing craft still continues today in many countries around the world. By definition, the term 'white witchcraft' certainly does include all the shades and colours of the rainbow, but I still always have a little chuckle (oh, let's face it, sometimes a really big cackle) whenever some novice magicians want to know what on earth could make me such a 'good' witch. Luckily I've had a fair bit of experience at actually living the full-on life of a witchy woman and I know for sure that no matter what fads may come and go, I am always going to be 'good' at what I do—especially when I feel like being very, very naughty.

You see, it's all about your intent and knowing where and when to use your different powers of enchantment and God/dess energies.

To put it really simply, once a real witch has done enough work on shedding some 'light' on her inner self and she knows that her instincts are honed and ready, she gains an enormous sense of her own magical power. She's learning to love all aspects of her nature, including bringing some healing energy in and out of the shadows; so she knows when it feels right to heal or hex, strike or stroke, and pretty much do what her own magical free will and intuition tells her.

Your intent is like a guiding light – it's a superjet that carries your Magic to its purpose.

A magical master can still do all of this fun stuff I like to call 'voodoo therapy' or 'sorcery for stress' without feeling uptight about it, because their magical decision is always based on a balanced view of the situation and it's really all about the 'good' intent, like self-defence, honouring grief, healing yourself or others (or just 'cause it feels so damn good to let it all out and be incredibly wild and wikid for a day).

And of course, a good ol' belly laugh never hurt anyone, and is especially helpful in blowing away the cobwebs of bitterness and magically dissolving leftover anger and sadness.

Witch or Wizard?

You have probably heard the saying 'there is a little bit of witch in every woman'. Well, that is absolutely right—and there are a few gorgeous goddesses thrown in for good measure too. Every woman has been equipped since birth with feminine intuition and witchy goddess power. These are natural instincts that directly align with a woman's highly developed emotional awareness and the necessary 'all-seeing' eye of a future mother and elder.

But let's not forget the males of the species, who are also called 'witches'. ('Warlock' is a misunderstood name and is rarely used these days.) Men sometimes—well, often, actually—get the short end of the stick when it comes to recognition of their own natural sensitivities, intuition and power. Being a female witch who has studied with a real live Man of Magic and met some very sensitive and intuitive male witches, I definitely consider that Witchcraft is not nor has ever been an exclusively female domain. Men and women are equal in the practice of the Craft. We need to accept and love male energy as part of the important duality and natural laws of life. Without it, true Magic is only half as effective. Just as a man needs to discover and strengthen his feminine and nurturing side, a woman gains power by discovering and strengthening her maleness and assertive masculine energy.

There is duality, male and female, yin and yang, black and white, positive and negative, in everything.

I've included a number of spells in the god and goddess section than can help empower you with the strong warrior and passionate male energies, as well as align you with both the yin and yang, male and female aspects of the Universe.

When it comes down to it, however, your ancient heritage is far more important than your chromosomal make-up in the world of Magic.

Whatever awakened your

spirit as a seeker and

set you on your path and

whatever first inspired

your journey into Magic

is correct and perfect for you

Your Ancient Heritage

Real Witches don't worry too much about certificates of Craft lineage or whether or not they had a Gypsy grandmother way back when.

Every one of us on this planet is a magical and spiritual being. We are all born with a magical heritage and a direct link to the Ancient Ones. Because you are an Ancient One—an eternally evolving soul moving through lifetimes … remembering, changing and remembering again.

Among the diversity, there seems to be one common connection between all traditions and paths into Magic and witchcraft, and that is the feeling of a deep spiritual connection to the old Wise Ones, and our respect and admiration for them, their knowledge and wisdom, and their spellcraft.

'Listening' to your dreams can be a great way of keeping in touch with your 'old' soul.

My own ancient self is never very far away during sleep and waking hours, and sometimes it actually jumps right out and takes me by the hand into my past lives. When I first started working on this book, I started having a strong 'vision' dream. I was out on a great plain sitting next to a fire in the misty, cold night air. When I looked around I saw that I was part of a big circle consisting of old grandmothers and younger women of all different races. Next to me were old Native American grandmothers, as well as Caucasian, African and Asian women, and what appeared to be a number of fur-clad women of Eskimo descent. I had this dream for a few nights in a row but the very last night I had it, one of the women stood up and crossed over the circle to me and gave me a warm hug, as if we'd known each other for a long time. Then we said goodbye with the words: 'Sister, we'll meet again through the mists of time.'

A couple of days later I was on the internet, holding a live chat with the members of my virtual magic circle, when as often happens, a brand-new member came on line and started to introduce herself. This in itself was not at all unusual but for some reason my heart started pumping loudly when I saw the name 'Delfina Rose, Native American Shamaness' written on the computer screen. For a split-second I was transported to that same dream circle of magical women. As I came back again—a heartbeat later—to 'real time', I read her message. She spoke about her Native American Shaman and Irish background and stories of her own circle of elders, including the grandmothers in her tribe. I felt my ancient self and my inner voices singing so loudly to me, that I took the very unusual step of asking this 'virtual' stranger to contact me off line, to see if she had picked up any similar 'voice' callings and vibrations.

Delfina, being the Shamaness and experienced magician that I have since found her to be, also had absolutely no doubts that our 'accidental' meeting was something of great meaning to us both—especially since she'd had a similar vision a while before. We have since spoken about what this re-awakening means and have both done separate rituals to go back and meet ourselves again—to help us discover the project we set ourselves all those aeons ago. Now that the mists are lifting the time is here, we are planning to do some type of project together and will meet most probably in her healing centre in Arizona. Whatever work our ancient selves have in mind for us, we will incorporate much of our dual visions and training with our elders into some type of joint mission. This seems to be just one of the many tasks my ancient self has already set down for me to do both alone and with other old souls.

Many witches today want to follow a similar spiritual path to the Ancient Magicians, and many of us either have 'memories' or a strong sense of what the Old Ones knew and understood.

For some of us, it may even seem like a re-awakening of our old training.

For those of us who believe in the eternity of the spirit, there is the follow-on logic that a naturally adept practitioner of Magic could simply be carrying on his or her role and path from a previous lifetime.

In the quantum world—which the old alchemists and witches knew about and worked with long before the word was even invented—and using meditation techniques and through experience, you may start to find that there is no difference between past, present and future.

You may come to understand that anyone can instantly connect with and access these ancient ways of knowing.

In other words, you can learn to bend time and space, to travel to other dimensions and be instantly connected to an old Druid as he walks you—his apprentice—through an ancient Irish grove; or be sitting in a philosophy class listening to Plato himself; or spend a few hours in a Hermetic School of Magic.

And, who knows, you may even be able to plug into the actual thoughts and living memories of that ancient philosopher or master magician.

In Magic, nothing is impossible! It is really just a matter of spending time learning and applying the natural laws of the universe on a daily basis.

We are the ancestors. We are the Wise Ones. We retain the living memories of them, as we learn how to remember.

Some people actually have flashbacks of who they were in a past life, and there are spells and rituals you can perform to help get a clearer view of your previous incarnations (I've included one in Part Three).

There are other ways, too, to connect with your ancient knowledge, which is a big part of what being a witch is all about.

The Re-awakening Process

Learning the first steps in Magic is really a re-awakening to what your spirit already knows. That is why you have been attracted to it, because your spirit recognises it and feels familiar—at home—with this knowledge and way of looking at life.

The paradox is that this knowledge is never exactly the same for each person. We don't have to reinvent the wheel, because it is all there for us to access in these ancient philosophies and spiritual paths.

But during the natural evolution process, you do add your own unique perceptions and consciousness to this ancient wisdom. And through you a new way of understanding and, eventually, imparting this knowledge may be born.

This is the way that knowledge evolves naturally and is passed on to future generations. But every Witch will follow these steps in their own unique way and time.

'All that has been will be again but never the same.'

Fenris, the Master Druid

The Three Stages

There appear to be three clear stages involved in attaining magical knowledge that, given enough time and study, most Witches will go through.

- The first stage involves recognising your latent and natural ability. This includes the initial years spent searching for a suitable path, guides, spiritual teachers or apprenticeship.

- The second step occurs in the middle years which are spent in continuous study and daily application of the magical knowledge as you grow and mature.

- The third step is where you reach a level of maturity and mastery in your path. In this stage you naturally become a co-creator and may wish to teach or to find some other way to pass the knowledge that you have acquired on to others.

But to begin with, more about setting that whole wheel in motion.

Making Natural Connections

When I was just a young kid, several years before I joined a Druid's Circle, I began searching for ways to keep awakening and strengthening my inner Magic. And one of the best ways that I found was to spend a lot of time in nature and taking the time to really look at the beautiful world around me. You see, being a Witch and applying your Magic is not just about specific techniques or rituals and defined doctrines, rules and redes. It is really a spiritual way of life, an inner journey, where you are learning to know and understand yourself, and to 'see' the world around you for the truly magical and miraculous place it is.

I vividly recollect the time I spent in my grandmother's garden as a small child. It was a carefully tended English garden—a paradise of old world scents, of lavender and roses. It backed onto a National Park where I explored hidden mossy caves and swam in freshwater streams along with slippery tadpoles. I was surrounded by an abundance of almost fluorescent native bushflowers, wild mushrooms and smelly, sticky toadstools—all of which I put to magical use, pulling them apart and mixing and mushing them to make strange potions used in secret rituals for the many sprites and faeries I communed with daily.

Through my natural childlike wonder and innocence, I discovered an important truth of witchcraft: that even though certain rituals and ancient techniques are valuable to learn and important to know, the most basic, simple things—such as sitting or lying under a tree (they don't call us 'tree huggers' for nothing), feeling its energy and life force and connecting with the earth under your body and feet—are a vital part of it.

Doing this can begin to align you with some of the natural laws of Magic as well as the wonderful Elements such as Earth.

Remember the old expression 'knock on wood'? This comes from old magicians, like the Druids, who would knock on an oak tree to contact the tree spirits.

Being outdoors, feeling the soft breeze on your face and practising deep breathing techniques and meditation can directly align you with the element of Air; doing so on a beach or in the sun aligns you with Water or Fire.

If you'd like to perform magic rituals to get in touch with the natural elements Earth, Air, Water or Fire, I've given you the guidelines and incantations for each in Part Three of this book. Using them, you can align yourself with the chosen element and be able to invoke the solidness of the earth beneath you, the lightness and freedom of the breeze, the might of the seas, or the vitality of the sun, for example.

You will find that the more you practise these simple rituals, the more connected with your inner Magic and that of the universe you become.

The most simple and natural things in life are usually the most profound and Magical.

Your spirit is eternal and is connected with all knowledge and wisdom in the universe. Your own mind and body contain the same elements as the stars, the planets, the ancient cosmic dust, as well as the elements and memories of all intelligence and genius, all that has ever been and will ever be—past, present and future.

Get Into a Good Head Space

A real witch should be well read and mentally active—after all, it's our mind that really does the focusing and application of true Magic. So you should be constantly exercising, training and strengthening your brain power. The more you train your mind, the better a magician you become. And that includes practising both creative and logical thinking.

A witch should never become 'one-eyed' or stuck in one point of view. You should be able to see the many different facets in everything—in people, opinions and everything around you.

Paradoxes are everywhere. Whatever truth you discover, the opposite is also true.

Read and learn about as many different philosophies and histories as you can. Don't learn just about Wicca or Druids, witches and spell-casters. Look into both modern and ancient science. Read the ancient Greek classics and Roman legends, and the writings of ancient philosophers and great minds of the past. Investigate the modern psychologists and visionaries such as Carl Jung and Joseph Campbell as well.

It's a step-by-step process, and even after 10, 20 or 30 years of study, you'll find that the most important step is to keep learning to 'know' yourself and look at the world and others in a

nonjudgmental and loving way. If you can do that, then most other processes will follow naturally at their own pace and in their own time.

Once you begin to understand the inner meaning of the rituals and various forms of practice, you will actually begin to go beyond the more set and defined forms and techniques and into the higher source of the Craft.

One of the strange paradoxes you can't help but find when studying the ancient lores of Magic is that the more you become aware of the deep psychology and forgotten meanings behind these old rituals and ancient practices, the more you see just how mutable, flexible and alive in the 'here and now' the core of it really is. It can be as fresh and new for us as it was when our ancestors first discovered these magical techniques many thousands of years ago.

This is why I'm not averse to the ways of the Craft moving out of the broom closet—I don't have any fear of it losing its mystery and wonder to me or others because the more I learn, the more mysterious and magical it all becomes. The knowledge actually helps you to appreciate the mystery and enchantment of every-thing—not just the spells and rituals, the 'high ceremonial' part of it, but also the everyday, mundane, simple things in life; they all become a part of the great Magic ceremony of being alive.

It's wondrous, and no matter how long you study, you can never get bored because there is so much more to know. Your mental ability expands and your overall tolerance level rises so you find that you *want* to know and keep learning more.

You'll probably find that you become addicted to reading books as well. So don't say I didn't warn you! Every mature-age witch I know is an incredible hoarder of information and usually has a collection of books—old and musty and brand-spanking new—that would make the National Library jealous.

The learning never ends. Even if you eventually become a teacher of Magic, you will remain a lifelong student. I look at my father, for instance, who was one of my first spiritual teachers. At 70 he is having another fresh burst of mental activity and mind expansion, which is truly amazing. He's writing a book trilogy based on his own theory of the meaning of life, and is still looking at the world through the eyes of a young discoverer. It's a great thing to look forward to. If we start early, we witches can look forward to many years of wonder and passion in life.

The more you study the world through ancient wisdom, the more you see the Universe through the eyes of a child.

See Part Three for the Cosmic Awakener, which will help open up your power of mind, and let you embrace the free-spirited witch within.

The elixir of magic is freedom,
And there lies a key to its alchemy for you.
Try and lock its golden light into just one box – and it instantly disappears from view.

Witchy Wild and Free

Trying to fit witchcraft into just one pathway is too narrow a concept for any Master Magician or Real Witch.

Just like Mercury, the ancient god Hermes who is Magic's favourite son, Magic and witchcraft are by their very nature wild, free, slippery and hard to pin down. And most witches are also freedom-loving individuals with strong natural spirits—they are as wild and untameable as any birds in the forest or lions in the jungle.

We are gypsies, with questioning minds and independent souls, though we may choose to stay and sit around the fire for a time, absorbing the wisdom of a spiritual master.

And we may study and respect different magical techniques and follow ancient guidelines and teachings—we don't need strict doctrines and religious dogma to show us what real Magic is. For we are already 'One' with the Universal god/goddess and feel a great love for the natural world around us.

The essence of Magic is inspired through a free and unhindered spirit. It is being able to let your spirit roam where it wills, feel what it wills, be what it wills. The secret of Magical Mastery is to do the above within a well-balanced and observant perspective.

This is a spiritual path as well as a philosophy, a way of looking at science, mathematics, nature and the universe. To many, it is also their choice of religion.

All combined, it is an ancient path; but it is also a path of modern knowledge that can help us understand and walk right into the future, to

look into what we and future generations on earth are going to be facing.

To be a Real Witch is an ever-evolving spiritual path that travels side by side with science, our physical health, our environment on earth, as well as our healthy sexuality and artistic expression.

It's about becoming a renaissance person and all-round human being capable of understanding and handling anything you set your mind to and, very importantly, allowing your neighbour their freedom to do the same.

Before we go on to the next chapter, here is another 'crafty' secret I'd like to reveal to you. You can all be the brightest of stars because every one of us is living in an enchanted paradise of golden opportunities. You're overflowing with so many wonderful gifts that the angels had to put them all in a cosmic bank for you. Now on the next pages, I'd like to give you some more enchanted keys to help open up that heavenly deposit box of yours, so you can really start making withdrawals from the endless well of Power and Magic.

magic
101

All you need to know to get started ~

How does a spell work? ~

Magical tools ~

Chants and incantations ~

Casting a circle ~

Your indoor temple ~

What's in a name? ~

Magic ways and means ~

Crystal power ~

Magic moments, seasons and times ~

part two

All you need to know to get started

Now that I have shared some of my magical training and given you some thoughts on what being a Real Witch is all about, I would like to show you what I know to be some of the essential tools and 'secret' keys to spellcasting and Magic.

Of course there are many other tools and methods in the Craft, but the following techniques are designed to give either a novice magician or an experienced Crafter some tried and true and unique hints as well as a way into the type of magical practice that has seen me through thick and thin and produced some spectacular results for both me and my inner circle over the years. Within this section you will also see the continuing 'practical and mystical' theme I spoke about earlier, and this is to help you absorb the fact that the most successful sorcery is always done with a combination of the mystical, esoteric themes, and the actual, physical action.

A great piece of witchy advice I would like to give you is: if you can use even some of these magical essentials, along with getting actively involved in your everyday work and relationships with the same type of 'get up and go', then the world can really be your enchanted oyster.

How Does a Spell Work?

Rituals and Magic spells are beautifully creative events that can be as overtly ceremonial and theatrical or as simple and direct as you desire them to be.

Whatever style of ceremony you choose, a spell needs to be as workable in the physical world as it is in the metaphysical. I like to use a combination of Occult techniques, depending on what type of spell I intend to cast. But whichever I choose, I always take into account the environment around me and what methods can be applied to the space I am working in.

For example, I might be out of broomsticks and want to work some Magic on a jet plane as I'm flying over the two Hemispheres, or I might want to connect with the elements in the middle of a desert with no tools except my own 'skyclad' body and willing mind, the earth firm beneath my feet and the heavens soaring above me!

An excellent ritual I have for both such occasions is called 'the Universal Compass' and you can use it any time and anywhere to help you connect with the major elements and all the directions of the world.

Not only does a Magic spell work by intent and the power of your thoughts, the alignment of your body, mind and spirit is also important to its effectiveness. All three of these aspects of yourself can be brought together by:

- deep breathing and meditation;
- letting go of nervous desire and impatience; and
- being consciously aware of your connection to the eternal universe.

Don't just believe it can happen, know it and see that it already has.

All aspects of the universe, including yourself—your mind, body and spirit—are connected; we are all energy. Everything we see around us is the physical manifestation of thought, and your thoughts have the power to

change the atmosphere of your mind, which can in turn change the dynamic of the atmosphere around you.

Nothing is ever destroyed or disappears entirely – everything is energy, and energy can only be transformed.

To create the right environment within and around you before a spell is cast, cleanse your aura and the space or room you will be using for spellcasting. This can be done very simply by spending some quiet time alone and calming your energies through meditation and deep-breathing exercises. If possible, you can bathe or take a shower to help wash away built-up stress.

You might like to perform your rituals 'skyclad' (what we witches call being naked). At other times you might want to wear a special robe that you only use for magical workings. What's best is to wear what feels the most comfortable and right for you.

Magical Tools

Most Magic charms use tools like candles, crystals, aromatic oils and herbs and spices, as well as spoken words and incantations. Why?

You can use these magical tools for both practical uses—as a source of light or heat, for their medicinal qualities, or to assist focus and concentration—and because each herb, colour, scent and incantation has its own esoteric use and unique vibration—a magical resonance that enhances the power of your spell, just like a musical instrument enhances a song.

Imagine when playing a guitar, for instance, a particular string is plucked and gives off a particular note—a wave of energy that you not only hear, but *feel* physically and emotionally as well. When the strings are strummed together in a chord, the different notes merge and create energy that enriches the atmosphere and causes a shift of emotions in people who are close by.

In the same way, because we are living in a quantum universe of overlapping space and time, you can also affect the object or person you are focusing your Magic on, no matter how far away they are on the planet.

The esoteric vibrations of colours, for example, are commonly used in Magic. Using a red candle in a spell, for instance, suggests passion and energy, while a blue candle inspires tranquillity and peace. A complete list of candle colours and their esoteric meaning appears on the following pages. The same applies to herbs and incense that can be used in spells. If you want to bring on prosperity, for example, you could use nutmeg or sage, or if your spell or ritual has a purifying intention, eucalyptus, vanilla or thyme could be used. Following is a comprehensive list of herbs and incense and their esoteric meanings.

Candle Colours
and Their Esoteric Meaning

BLUE: success, peace, tranquillity and protection

BROWN: animal Magic, environment and grounding

GOLD: the Sun, wealth and royalty

GREEN: luck, growth, prosperity and healing

ORANGE: creativity, health and attraction

PINK: love, friendship, femininity and gentleness

PURPLE: spirituality, psychic ability and enchantment

RED: passion, lust, energy, vitality and strength

SILVER: mysticism, the Moon and prosperity

WHITE: truth, purity, meditation and spiritual protection

YELLOW: concentration and mental ability

Herbs, Spices and Incense
and Their Esoteric Meaning

ALLSPICE: spiritual vibrations and strengthens in any ritual

BASIL: wealth, love and fertility

BAY: protection, clairvoyance and good fortune

CARNATION: healing, vitality and friendship

CINNAMON: luck, love and prosperity

CLOVE: memory, eyesight and attraction

EUCALYPTUS: healing and cleansing

FRANKINCENSE: high Magic, protection and purification

GARDENIA: arousing, aphrodisiac and passion

GARLIC: banishing and protection

JASMINE: spiritual love, happiness and erotic feelings

JUNIPER: safety, protection, love and affection

LAVENDER: attraction, sexuality, beauty and purification

MARJORAM: happiness, cleansing and affection

MINT: clear sight, energy and cleansing

MUGWORT: protection and powerful goddess energies

NUTMEG: prosperity, attraction and clairvoyance

ORANGE: harmony and a happy atmosphere

ROSE: love, passion and friendship

ROSEMARY: purification, healing, good fortune and high Magic

SAGE: prosperity, cleansing and good health

SANDALWOOD: mental ability, meditation and tranquillity

THYME: clairvoyance, protection and purification

VANILLA: purity, affection and feminine attraction

Chants and Incantations

When casting a Magic spell, your own voice and the words you speak are a very important part of the ritual, especially since your voice triggers certain vibrations and resonances in the universe. The old Celtic Druids and Bards considered poetry, music and the spoken word to be full of great sorcery and spent many years honing their skills in wordcraft and songs—which might explain why so many of us witches are creative writers and singers.

On the pages that follow are a few of the simple incantations I have used over the years. Some of them were passed down to me from my Elders, and I created the others. They have worked very well for me, so please feel free to use them as often as you need.

When you get a feeling for the way the structures and rhythms of the incantations work, add your own lines and use them to practise with.

After a while you will begin to see the deep connections and high Magic behind the wordcraft, poetry and music.

It really is inspiring and lots of fun, and the more you practise it, the better you become.

The Rhythm of Life

Through my 'Bardic' family background and Druidic training, I've come to discover quite a few handy secrets about the magical ways of words, rhythms and even song melodies.

Getting to know how different word and music rhythms can cause different effects in spellcasting can take quite a bit of time and study, but here are some important keys to the understanding of it, and if you practise with these types of rhythm techniques,

you won't be a 'slave' to the rhythm, but a Magical master of it.

There are a variety of styles to enchanted rhythms. The first one is the one-liner; this is an ancient single-beat 'power stroke' that can be used on its own as a spell, or can be added to the end of a longer spell to give power and resolution. In modern terms, you could say that this is the 'pay-off' line and interestingly enough, the one-liner is the style that's often used in modern affirmations and even commercial advertising. (There may very well have been some witchy minds working overtime when someone came up with the great 'power stroke' of 'Share the Spirit' for the incredibly successful Sydney Olympics.)

But for our purposes, we can use magical one-liners such as the tried and true 'power strokes': 'It *Will* Be So' or 'So *Mote* It Be' or the slightly longer 'So *Shall* My Request Be Heard'. Note that there is an emphasis on the action words in the line to help push the rhythm along.

The most popular of the incantations are the rhyming kind that usually have about three or four lines. The words will tell a little story about the type of spell it is, and the intent or purpose of the charm.

For instance, you can probably guess instantly the intention of the spell below, even without me explaining it to you. Note the all important 'pay-off' line at the end that signifies the intent and purpose of the spell.

> 'This candle is my burning love
> As bright as the sacred Sun,
> May this flame warm your soul
> And let us soon be one.'

The above spell is in a 4/4 rhythm, which is a popular and joyous rhythm used to enhance an incantation or a magical song. You can also play around with 3/4 rhythms, which are more waltzy and can be more poignant too. It is said that the ancient High Priestesses of Delphi also made great use of all rhythms and music for sorcery—especially the 3/4 and 4/4 beats—to get everyone excited and inspired.

You don't always have to use poetry or rhyming words to be effective. Sometimes you can use just a few very meditative or strong lines that get your point across and are more like affirmations.

'Let all impurities be cast from me
with this cleansing breath.'

Then you can add a more resolving 'power stroke' line with something like:

'O Blessed Be' or 'Thank you, my Goddess'

And finally, here is a very old key to effective Bardic spells and chants that has been used for many centuries—the use of the magical Quatrane. This is where you do a four-liner, and then add an extra 'power stroke' and 'pay-off' line at the end—sending your incantation and final intent zooming off into the Universe.

Here's an example of it that I used for a spell called the Cheapskate Charm which appeared in Nice Girl's Book of Naughty Spells. (I've since heard from many readers who have had great success with this one!)

'While money is owed to those who wait,
Bills pile up and confusion reigns,
Your conscience shall prick
When I repeat this plea,
Allow what is mine to return to me.'

Readymade Incantations

To Awaken Love For Yourself

'I now let go of unhappiness and stress
and I open my mind, body and spirit
to receive the wisdom of the Universe.'

or

'I am content in my own Universe,
I create and give love and friendship
and I will learn to know my inner self.'

To Attract a Soulmate

Concentrate on the moon or a star
that attracts your attention and think loving thoughts.

'With these Magic words I begin my spell
Hear me, oh mystic star, hear me well.
Let your Magic light send me the love of my life.'

To Bring Back an Ex-lover

Picture yourself and this person back together
and happy again.

'Each time you wake,
each road you take,
you shall be feeling my love.'

For Getting a Job or Success in Business

'I feel it, trust it and I shall be it,
Now luck and good fortune shine on us all.'

For Peace and Harmony

'Love before me,
love beside me,
love behind me,
bring peace, harmony and truth.'

To Expel Bad Luck and Negative Energy

'All the bad energy is now gone,
I see reflected only pure light and affection.'

To Boost Self-esteem

'Deep within me, my soul is my guide,
I shall put away my fears and know
that I deserve to love and be loved.'

For Help With Legal Problems and Court Cases

'Spirit of success and justice
surround me with good fortune.'

To Heal a Broken Heart

'Oh shimmering star,
weave your magic spell tonight.
Help me feel my soul within,
so my wonderful new life can now begin.'

Song of Kullerone (sung in the key of E minor)

If you are musically inclined, writing chants and poetry is a great way to stimulate your songwriting too. Here is an example of one of my own compositions that was written for a mystical rock opera, about a lost enchanted island called Kullerone.

Fair maiden waiting, gold rings in her hair, her heart is breaking
White knights are riding, a sword in their hand,
Their last stand for Kullerone,
Sorcerer weaves his way into their soul,
Memories will fade
Lovers are weeping while legends are made on the shores
Of Kullerone,
Island alone, I hear you calling
O come take me home,
My Kullerone.
Put out to sea in boats made of pearl
Hear the winds howl
Sail far from the land where Magic was born
Away from our own.

Our Kullerone
Island alone, we hear you calling
O come take us home,
Kullerone.
(REPEAT ABOVE CHORUS)
O my beth, O my shay,
no traces or a sign,
you shall remain between the ways,
'Til I come to make you mine.
(WHISPER ABOVE CHANT UNTIL FADE)

Deborah Gray, 1983

Learning the first steps in Magic is really a re-awakening to what your spirit already knows.

Casting a Circle

When you cast a circle, you create your own magical environment and a focus of cosmic power within and around you.

Whether you cast a circle, a square, pyramid or star, you are not creating a shield or barrier from outside forces. You are creating a psychological space that can help take you out of the 'normal' mundane world that you interact with every day, and into the mystical, metaphysical world.

You don't perform circle 'boundary' rituals to switch off or block spiritual energies. You do it because you are trying to join, connect and be 'one' with the infinite energies.

Appreciating the Law of the Paradox

What I am about to tell you next is very important to your practice as a witch and is in accordance with ancient Occult knowledge and High Magic techniques.

If it doesn't make a lot of sense to you at first, don't worry; just take the next piece of information in and know that when you are ready, its meaning will become clear.

Every action we do and experience in life has more than one meaning and more than one outcome and reaction.

An experienced witch works with the knowledge of both the physical and the metaphysical world, and we also work with the knowledge of the paradox—which exists in *both* the physical and the metaphysical worlds.

The paradox of the circle ritual and the 'boundary' you are creating is that at the same time as you are creating a circle 'boundary'—you are also creating a circle of 'no boundaries'. You are listening with both your conscious and subconscious mind to the universal mind, which also exists in a space of 'no boundaries'.

Raising Power

Many witches always cast a circle or a spiral to help focus and raise energy before they begin a spell, but this is not essential practice. What you choose to do depends on your own instincts and traditions.

There are countless ways to raise energy. Some traditions cast their circle by calling up the four elements and the 'Watchtowers', and then may raise up a 'cone of power', while others believe in calling on protective spirits or angelic energies. Others again like to work with fairy or 'Faery' energies or Nature sprites or the different pantheons of ancient gods and goddesses.

Whatever methods you use, work at your own pace and try out different approaches one at a time to see what works—what 'resonates' magically for you. What works for you will often depend on what type of person you are. Maybe you are more of a cerebral type of person who feels more inspired by being alone or sitting in a circle with others, quietly focusing your mind and body with meditative rituals. Or you may get a lot of excitement and magical value from trying out the more physically involving rituals which can incorporate dancing, beating drums, singing and chanting (which can be done both alone or with a magical group).

The point is there is no 'right' or 'wrong' way to connect with the source of Magic and to raise up energy —

the only right thing is whether you are getting inspired from the ritual and feeling it happening.

Especially when you are just starting out in the Craft, it's best to work with rituals that inspire you in a more positive and uplifting way as well as those that help you connect with the 'oneness' of yourself and the eternal universe.

Begin with rituals you relate to and understand. There's no point in attempting ceremonies that are so full of complicated symbols and language that you don't really know what you're trying to do and lose sight of what you are trying to achieve.

Remember to trust in the Universe so you can be fully open and relaxed. There's far less chance of you getting in touch with your witchy nature if you are fearful or cast your circle thinking you need to protect yourself from entities or 'outside forces'. Putting up psychological barriers will only create unwanted tension and that won't allow you to fully connect or achieve anything much at all, except perhaps to give yourself a stress headache, which ain't too magical.

Even if you don't have a more experienced person to perform rituals with, you can always get in touch with your own 'wise wizard' inside yourself.

You can help dissolve any fears and tensions by performing really simple meditation and de-stressing spells, and then just take your time feeling comfortable with whatever you are doing. Don't worry, you can't hurt yourself or raise up any unwanted energies just because you accidentally say something backwards or don't do something at the perfect time—the universal energies don't ever judge you like that.

Circle of Light

This wonderful ritual is one of my favourite ways of casting a circle and raising a spiral of energy. It is for focusing and invoking a sense of growth, attraction and abundance. It can help put you into a meditative and responsive state wherever you are, and *connect your spiritual and physical energies to the Universal forces around, above and below you.*

It requires no external tools, but is still one of the most powerful and ancient rituals you can do. Perform it day or night, including whenever you feel your psychic and physical energies need a boost or to enhance the power of a spell.

Find a comfortable and private space, either outdoors or indoors, and stand, breathing calmly. Loosely cup your hands together in front of you so that you can see the palms of both of your hands. Look closely at the centre of both of your hands and look at the tiny lines on your palms. Observe how there appears to be a curved space that is perfect for holding a small sphere.

Keep looking until you visualise that small sphere softly glowing in your hands, and in your mind's eye, imagine that it contains a mini universe that is shimmering with thousands, then millions, of tiny suns and stars, which are starting to merge into a mini galaxy of light. The more you look into this cosmic sphere, the more you really see this mini universe which has its own galaxy of stars circling slowly around inside it in a clockwise direction.

Feel the power and energy of that mini galaxy as it starts to spiral up through your entire body. When you are feeling uplifted and revitalised, start turning on the spot to the right, in a clockwise direction. Spin once

or twice in a circle and joyously fling the light sphere away from you and watch the sphere dissolve into the atmosphere, scattering those thousands of tiny stars to surround yourself with your own expanding galaxy and circle of light.

Why Clockwise or 'Deosil'?

In the above spiral of power you turn to the right because it's an ancient symbol and psychological trigger for going forward and moving towards the light. Think about the old saying 'putting your right foot forward' and why in most cultures we greet each other by shaking the right hand. Even our clocks, our precious time keepers, turn 'clockwise' to the right, and no matter where you are on Earth, if you stand facing the North at dawn, the first life-giving rays of the Sun will rise in the East and shine on your right side.

'Deosil' is from the old Scottish term 'Deiseal', meaning 'turning to the right' and is also a Craft term for clockwise or 'sunwise'. Because the Sun's energy gives us light and life, while the Moon is a cold and mysterious planet with a 'dark' side, humans, plants and most other living creatures naturally turn towards the sunlight to 'wake up', grow and blossom. The left side, turning in the opposite direction towards the Moon and night, helps us dream, rest and travel through the more mysterious side of us. Through both evolution and culture, this 'sunwise' and 'moonwise'—right and left action—became a very strong part of the belief system. Throughout Europe and in many other parts of the world, right-turning, clockwise rituals like the one above have been performed for thousands of years and are magically effective in the most universal and profound way.

There are some left-handed and Southern Hemisphere witches who prefer casting 'forward motion' and 'attraction' circles in an anticlockwise

66

'widdershins' direction. And hey, that is perfectly cool if works for them, but I personally wouldn't recommend you cast a 'forward' circle in an anticlockwise direction, regardless of what country or Hemisphere you might be working in. Not because anything drastic can happen, but simply because our genetic and psychological adherence to these left and right actions is often too ingrained, and it can get confusing to swap around.

Anticlockwise Rituals

The left-hand side has received a bit of bad publicity in times gone by. Many natural left-handers were forced to write with their right hands, and even the Latin name for left, 'sinister', meant 'dark' and 'evil'. But this is just superstition, and casting an anticlockwise circle to trigger your left side does not have such a purely negative connotation in Magic. It is about subconsciously turning to the direction of the Moon and the night. The anticlockwise circle is cast for going backwards into the past, for cleansing a space or ridding yourself of leftover stress, or working with the deep and the more mysterious witchy energies and your moonshadow side for a change.

The following widdershins, anticlockwise ritual can be used for clearing away negative energies and past worries and for 'washing' a magical space in readiness for further spellcasting and rituals.

Instead of visualising a sphere of light, imagine you are holding a bowl of water. And as you look into it, start breathing deeply in and out. With each breath, imagine the water is drawing out all your doubts and fears about yourself. As it absorbs those heavy and negative sensations, feel the water revitalise you and recharge you with a sense of inner calm and strength. Whenever you are ready, start spinning to the left, in an anticlockwise direction, flinging the imaginary bowl of water away from you. Watch it

flow into a beautiful velvety river of energy that dissolves into the atmosphere, washing over everything with a deep sense of spiritual cleansing and a feeling of release.

Closing the Circle

Some witches like to 'close circle' soon after they have finished casting their Magic and spells. On most occasions I like to retain at least some of the 'uplifting' and energised state of mind so I simply allow my energies to settle down naturally. I usually spend a few moments in quiet reflection and meditation at the end of each spell or ritual and perhaps say some relaxing words like:

'I now dissolve this circle of power and give thanks to the Universal God/dess',

Or I may choose to ground myself by sitting comfortably or lying down on either the floor, grass, rock or sand, and feeling the 'grounding' energy gently bringing me back down to earth and everyday reality.

Temple of the Four Winds

This magical stone circle was taught to me during my years of apprenticeship with the sorcerer Fenris. It is called the Temple of the Four Winds because it not only honours the power of the four winds but it is also built as a permanent circle of stones, in a similar way to a Druid's temple, and can be entered alone or with guests for meditation, special rituals or spells. If you have enough space outdoors, in your own backyard or terrace, you can build the circle whatever size you like, but if space is a problem you can build one that is just big enough for one or two people to stand or sit in and then keep it permanently set up as your special outdoor temple.

You will need to gather:

- a wooden stick (this will become your Magic Stang) 90 cm or more long (this can be a slim piece of any tree branch, a broom handle or a simple or ornate walking stick); you will also need to work out which end of the stick you choose to be the top and which is the bottom end
- some chalk or a can of white spray paint (optional)
- a measuring tape (optional)
- a number of pebbles or medium-sized stones (how many depends on how big you decide to make your circle)
- a basket or bag for the stones (optional)
- a cup of sea or rock salt

You can build this stone circle on any reasonably fine morning of the year, but the most powerful time to erect the temple is during summer when the sun is at its strongest peak (particularly the dawn of the Summer Solstice).

If you have already worked out from which direction the Sun rises in your area, then that's all you need to work out—where East is. If not, you will need to get a compass to work it out.

The day before you build your temple, look for a safe, quiet spot outside in your backyard, courtyard, or on an open air balcony (preferably where you can go and be undisturbed and relaxed). When you have found the perfect spot, meditate for a while to help cleanse your aura and settle your energies. Then work out the exact position and size you'd like your temple to be (the measuring tape can help here). Next draw a clockwise circle either in the earth with a stick, or with a piece of chalk on the ground, or you can use either a paint brush or can of spray paint. Around this stage you can also work out if you have enough stones or pebbles to build the temple. Do a test by placing your stones around the traced circle to see if you have enough. (The stones don't have to be touching each other; you can place them up to 30 cm apart if you don't want to collect too many). When you have finished your test and drawn or painted your circle, take away all the stones, and store them outside the circle (in a container or bag if you wish). Then pick up the cup of salt and walk just once around the traced circle in an anticlockwise (widdershins) direction, sprinkling the salt as you go, to cleanse the area. Next, leave the traced circle as it is overnight so the area can be charged by the energy of the Moon.

That night, before you go to sleep, set your alarm clock early so you can be ready to start building at least half an hour before sunrise. In the morning after you have had a quick wash you can either dress in some comfortable clothes or remain skyclad. Then go out and gather all the stones and the wooden stick, go back out into the centre of the circle and put the stones and the stick down in the middle. Sit nearby in a comfortable position facing East, and wait for the Sun to rise. As soon as you see the rays of the Sun lighting up the sky, pick up just your wooden stick, stand up, and walk over to the Eastern edge of the circle. Hold the stick with the top end pointing majestically up to the sky to be charged by the rays of the morning Sun and say out loud:

> 'Sacred rays of the Eastern Dawn, charge us now with glorious new beginnings and the fire of life.'

70

Then when you feel ready, walk slowly and evenly around the circle to the right, in a clockwise direction (Deosil) with the stick pointing to the ground in front of you—as if you are retracing the exact line of the circle and now charging it with the Sun's magical energy. Then when you have walked once completely around the circle you should end up back facing the sunrise in the Easterly position.

Remain facing the Sun with your arms raised to the sky. Breathe deeply in and out as you feel your lungs being cleansed with fresh air. Hold the stick once more up towards the sky, as you say this incantation with conviction:

> 'Gather now all four winds of East, North, South and West,
> blow from all corners of the Earth, Sun, sky, and sea.
> Now together we are as one as we cast this our circle of power.
> So Mote it Be.'

Next, walk back into the centre of the circle and tap the bottom end of the stick three times on the ground. Then lay the stick down and pick up as many stones as you can (take the container with you if you like) and start placing them one by one in a Deosil (clockwise) direction around the circle. If you need to go back into the centre and collect more stones, that's okay, just keep laying them all down in a clockwise direction until you have laid down an evenly spaced circle of stones.

When you have finally finished laying down the stones, go back and stand in the centre of your circle. Then pick up the wooden stick once again, turn on the spot and face the sunrise again. Hold the stick for the last time in the sky directly above you as you say:

> 'I call on the Lords of Light, the goddess Moon and Sun
> to honour this our temple of the four winds,
> for as long as it stands may this be
> a sacred space of Magic and eternal wisdom.
> O Blessed Be.'

Finish the ritual by tapping the ground again three times with the bottom end of the stick and then you may walk out of the temple in any direction. To 'lock up' the energies of the temple while you are away, stand outside it and say:

> 'Between the ways guards the Lords and Goddess of Light,
> we shall go with honour, merry meet, merry part
> and merry meet again.'

Make sure you bring anything left over from the ritual with you and keep your wooden stick in a safe place wrapped in a piece of silk, cotton or leather. Because your stick has been energised by the ritual, it is now called your 'Magic Stang' and it is to be used only by you (or a delegated person) and only when you want to go back and meditate or do some rituals in the temple.

Whenever you wish to re-enter the temple for meditation or for special rituals, re-open the magical doorway by standing outside any part of the circle holding your 'Magic Stang'. Tap the end of the stick on the ground three times and say:

> 'I open the ways to greet the blessing of the Lords and
> the Goddess of Light,
> Merry Meet.'

And then walk into the temple.

Once you have opened the magical doorway to the temple, you or any guests can walk in and out from any direction as much as you like. You can bring any spell items or decorations in and out with you and when you have finished your rituals, you or the delegated person are in charge of 'locking' the magical doorway up again with the previous closing ritual.

Don't be surprised if you keep finding your family pet curled up asleep inside it—or if your smallest child always seems to enjoy playing in the middle of this outdoor temple. There's no need to discourage it, as this happens simply because animals and children are naturally attracted to the circle's natural goddess and Faery vibrations. Their presence is always welcomed and only enhances the magical energies within.

A real witch lives a life filled with free spirited creativity, a passionate sense of love and the world, and a boundless love for Earth and Nature.

Your Indoor Temple

I like to think of my home as being an indoor temple, with not only rooms for rest, work and sharing food with my friends and family, but also with some special area within where no matter how deliciously chaotic and untidy the rest of the house may get, I always have my own 'sacred space' for weaving certain spells or to just sit quietly and meditate for a while. My sacred space and magical altar are near a window in my bedroom, where I have placed an old-fashioned dressing table and mirror and on which I have strewn all my favourite crystals and seashells and my collection of new and antique perfume bottles. Because I am quite an eclectic witch I am always on the lookout for new and interesting knickknacks and I also have a variety of candlesticks and magical tools, including a set of pewter chalices, a specially carved bone and crystal wand, and recently I found a small but exquisitely engraved ceremonial knife, which I now use as my 'Athame', and that, along with a plump little statue of the Laughing Buddha, takes pride of place amongst my collection.

There are lots of different ways to set up your own altar, and while some of the contemporary Craft traditions have very definite rules on which direction you should be facing and what specific tools you should have, I really think that the most enchanting altars are those that contain items you personally treasure, have made yourself, or have chosen because they have called out to you in a shop or a flea market stall and said:

'Buy me! I can help you make Magic!'

You can create an altar facing North, in the direction of Dreams and the Moon, or facing East, in the sacred direction of the rising Sun.

What's in a Name?

Magical names can be both inspiring and very useful in creating just the right energy for rituals and spellcasting. The name 'Belthane' is my own adaptation from the witchy festival 'Beltane' and I love to go by that name during my old coven's favourite celebration, Walpurgisnacht on April 30th, and during any of the Spring and Summer rituals, or simply when I feel like adding some extra 'sunshine' and a happy spring feeling into my life.

You don't have to rush out and choose a magical name at all if you don't want to, and funnily enough I have found that a lot of witchy folks I know seem to think that some of the most powerful names actually choose you. For instance, myself and quite a few of my magical friends were never Christened or given our birth names through a normal religious ceremony. Instead, each of us went through our first official 'naming ceremony' in very unusual and witchy circumstances. Like many coven-educated witches, I also have a secret Craft name that was given to me in my first ever naming ceremony or 'christening' by Fenris the Druidmaster (and I retain its power by keeping it secret and only using it whenever I want to make contact with him). My friend Athena was officially named for the first time in a feather and water ceremony by a Mexican Indian Shaman called Don Juan, who 'christened' her with the name 'Starwoman' in the 1970s. And it has certainly helped to resonate the perfect 'star' essence around her life and work. Athena also tells me that sometimes, when she feels she needs grounding, she calls herself 'Earthwoman' for a few hours—just to have a bit of rest from zooming around the planets. Names definitely resonate around you with their own energy and each name can inspire you in very different ways.

If you're in search of an enchanting name for your witchy work, then here's a short list of suggested names along with their magical vibrations and meanings.

Celtic and Gaelic names

FEMALE

- Aideen: Irish lover of the fairy man
- Aine: fair Queen
- Aislin: dream
- Ashore: loved one
- Brenna: raven maid
- Brigid: strong
- Calum: dove
- Cara: friend
- Darcy: dark one
- Duvessa: dark beauty
- Edana: little fire
- Fenella: fair
- Genevieve: magic sighs
- Gwyneth: white lady
- Keelia: beauty
- Rhiannon/Epona: witch and horse goddess
- Riona: queenly
- Rona: sea
- Sabia: goodness
- Shannon: little wise one
- Ula: jewel of the sea

MALE

- Ahern: lord of horses
- Arthur: noble
- Baird: ballad singer
- Bram: raven
- Calhoun: warrior
- Callum: messenger of peace
- Carlin: little champion
- Casey: brave
- Conlan: hero
- Dagda: strong wizard god
- Dallan: wise
- Devin: poet
- Donnovan: dark warrior
- Edan: fiery
- Forbes: wealthy and prosperous
- Galen: intelligent
- Gavin: white hawk
- Hogan: youthful and spirited
- Mahon: bear strength
- Morgan: sea's edge
- Murrough: sea warrior
- Niall: champion energy
- Sheridan: wild man
- Tiernan: lord

Greek names

FEMALE

- Amarantha: immortal
- Ambrosia: food of life
- Anastasia: one who will rise again
- Astra: starlike
- Calandra: lark and song
- Chloe: flowering
- Delphine: oracle of Apollo
- Dorissa: sea
- Ilona: light
- Iris: goddess of the rainbow
- Melanie: dark beauty
- Moira: goddess of destiny
- Penelope: the weaver
- Phoebe: moon goddess
- Theola: divine
- Trina: pure
- Ursa: she-bear
- Zandra: helper of humankind
- Zoe: life giving

MALE

- Ajax: eagle
- Alexander: great protector
- Cosmo: the world
- Darius: wealthy
- Homer: promise
- Jason: the healer
- Leander: lion man
- Orestes: mountain
- Orion: hunter
- Phalen: calms
- Sebastian: majestic
- Zeno: shining

Miscellaneous Cultures and Energies

- Adora: beloved one
- Aurora: golden energy
- Belinda: beautiful serpent
- Bellona: Goddess of War
- Blackthorn: protection
- Bluebird: great name to make you feel happy
- Bryony: balance
- Cerelia: Goddess of the Harvest
- Chantal: singer and enchantress
- Diana: goddess of the hunt
- Draco: dragon lover
- Faline: catlike
- Fayiana: dancer
- Goldenrod: Magical healer
- Hawthorn: an ancient and powerfully witchy name
- Heather: graceful and quietly powerful
- Leandra: lioness and leo aspects
- Lily and Lena: feminine and exotic temptress
- Lucretia: wealthy and clever herbalist
- Lumina: a good name for personal enlightenment
- Luna: Moon Goddess energy
- Lyra: bright star and musically bright
- Mahogany, Orchid and Rowan: great names for exotic looks; gives protection
- Maiea: Goddess of Springtime
- Maris: of the sea
- Portia: offering
- Risa: laughing one
- Sibyl: prophetess and fortune teller
- Terra: Goddess of the Earth
- Valora: strong and courageous

Enchanting Combinations
Male and female

- Aidan Nightwind
- Aldwyn Greenwood
- Annwyn Celestine
- Artemis Dreamweaver
- Astra Angel
- Axel Beowulf
- Axel Ra
- Beowulf Moonstone
- Bram Uther
- Bran Cerridwyn
- Bright Saffron
- Callista Rune Moonstone
- Dagda Avalon
- Danu Morag
- Dru Butterfly
- Druida East Elf
- Earth Serpent Ice
- Edain Maeve Bear
- Edris Arianrhod
- Eldritch Adrian
- Eldritch Osiris
- Eldritch Storm
- Elf-Arrow
- Erlic Danu

- Faery Bringer
- Gaia Rhiannon
- Gandalf Moonshadow
- Gold Cougar
- Gwydion Rain
- Gwyneth Tor
- Ipona Ariel
- Isis Rainbow
- Luna Mist
- Mab Feather Wynn
- Mahogany Wizard Boy
- Merlin Ice Glimmer
- Moonwoman Thunder Hawk
- Morgan Ariadne
- Mystic Silver
- Niamh Acorn
- Raven Moon Crow
- Sky Wolfe
- Star Weaver
- Tara North
- Thunder Angel
- Thunder Lugh Purple
- Western Sky Flame
- Winter Firestorm
- Wolverine Swordbringer

For further reading on this subject, I suggest you pick up a copy of the fantastic book The Complete Book of Magical Names by Phoenix McFarland.

Some names, such as High Priestess or Elder, are more like titles to describe a level of mastery and years of experience and hold a lot of weight behind them because they are ancient and have deep meanings. While such names are very useful, like any tool they should be used well, with deep respect and, in this case, only where necessary and appropriate.

Be discerning about people you might meet who, after just a year or two of study, call themselves names like Most Almighty Powerful One or Grand Highest Pooh-Bah Priestess. Magical names aren't meant to be used as a form of worship; if they are, sooner or later the effect will wear off.

It's a bit like that great scene in the Disney cartoon Fantasia where Mickey Mouse is the Sorcerer's apprentice and starts spinning some broom Magic from the Master's personal spell book. Before long, the spell's power gets away from him and he doesn't have enough knowledge or experience to turn it off again. For us as witches, using a name like High Priestess can be a bit like playing with that Magic from the Master's personal spell book; you could easily be playing out of your depth. Remember, these are ancient terms of mastery, so make sure you are ready for them.

They are powerful and the Magic within them comes with a big responsibility.

Ironically, one of the most experienced and clever witches I know, Leonora, who has been quietly practising the Craft for over 30 years and has lived and taught in a highly respected coven for most of that time, simply likes to call herself a 'witch' or a 'metaphysic'. When I asked her recently why she doesn't use the term High Priestess (and she has certainly earned the right to use it) and rarely dresses in her ceremonial robes during magical workshops, she replied, 'Because I want my students to know that they can do this on the bus.'

Whatever the case, by all means call yourself any mythical or magical term that inspires and appeals to you, but try not to use a name that weighs you down like an old suitcase and never lose your sense of humour about yourself.

As my old coven master used to always say, 'When two sorcerers meet, the one who isn't laughing isn't a sorcerer.'

Magic Ways and Means
Aroma Magic

Wonderful power springs from the aroma of flowers and plants, and magicians have been practising and perfecting the mystical art which we now call 'aromatherapy' for thousands of years. Each aromatic plant, fragrant flower and scented herb has its own essential qualities and scents that can be used in healing massages and baths, in oil burners or in Magic potions and lucky oils.

Many of the commonly used essential oils of aromatherapy are readily available from pharmacies and health food stores, but if you are really keen, you can distil your own floral and herbal essences. But to begin with, you can have lots of fun creating your own enchanted potions with just a few basic essential oils. It might be a good idea to read about the basics of aromatherapy before you begin; there are many books on the subject available in bookshops, new age stores and libraries. You can also simply choose an aroma based on a particular emotion or state of mind from the list of characteristics that follows, or read through the list of Essences for Every Occasion on the following page and pick an oil for its particular properties. The following is an esoteric guide to the use of a magical essence or herb.

Aroma Quick Finder

◉ Love: jasmine, gardenia, rose and neroli

◉ Lust: basil, cinnamon, ginger, neroli and ylang ylang

◉ Wealth: bergamot, mint, nutmeg and allspice

◉ Healing: rosemary, sandalwood and carnation

◉ Protection: basil, frankincense and lavender

◉ Money: clove and pine

◉ Tranquillity: lavender, marjoram, thyme and chamomile

◉ Uplifting: St John's wort (also good for nervous tension), bay and carnation

◉ High Magic blessing: benzoin, frankincense and rue

Essences For Every Occasion

◉ Eucalyptus: uplifting, cleansing, banishing

◉ Geranium: romance, antidepressant and cleansing

◉ Jasmine: spiritual love, serenity, beauty

◉ Lavender: soothes, heals, calms conflict

◉ Lemon: good fortune and power

◉ Marigold: healing, promotes tranquillity and peace

◉ Mimosa: add to jojoba oil for care of sensitive skin

◉ Mint: joyful, inspirational and energising

◉ Orange: healing, energy and love

◉ Petitgrain: healing and de-stressing

◉ Rose: love, passion and femininity

◉ Rosemary: sexuality, anxiety and stress

◉ Sandalwood: peace, meditation and cleansing

◉ Ylang ylang: sensuality and happiness

Crystal Power

Precious gems and crystals have been worn both for their beauty and their magical qualities since earliest recorded history. Some gems are known to absorb the warmth and moisture of the skin and many crystals can change colour in different light and atmospheres. Whether you wear them in elaborate necklaces and bracelets, or carry a single crystal in your pocket, their powers—mystical and legendary—are equally potent.

Birthstones

Birthstone Magic can be traced as far back as 4000 BC to the spellcasters of Memphis in Egypt who wore breastplates encrusted with special gems to protect and empower them with mystical energy.

One of the easiest ways to find your own birthstone is through the help of the stars. Look up your zodiac sign below, and when you have obtained the corresponding crystal, wash it in spring water mixed with a pinch of salt. Dry it well with a clean white cloth and keep it on your desk, altar, or in a magical box.

Hold your birthstone on a Full or New Moon in both hands and say:

> 'Stone of Beauty, fine to see, consecrated now to me,
> Help me well in time of strife.
> Bring good luck effectively,
> And as my will, so mote it be!'

84

Astrological Birthstones

- Aries: garnet
- Taurus: turquoise
- Gemini: agate
- Cancer: moonstone
- Leo: amber
- Virgo: carnelian
- Libra: lapis lazuli
- Scorpio: tourmaline
- Sagittarius: topaz
- Capricorn: malechite
- Aquarius: aquamarine
- Pisces: amethyst

Not only are many of these stones bright and alluring, but each also has its own special and enchanted attributes. To use a gem in a spell, choose whatever charm you would like to cast and wash the appropriate crystal in some spring water mixed with a pinch of salt. Dry the crystal well with a clean white cloth and keep your Magic crystal in your pocket, on your desk or somewhere nearby.

The following list outlines the properties of gems often used as charms and in spells.

Crystals and Their Properties

- Amethyst: for courage, emotional love, success
- Aventurine: attracts calming energy, luck, intelligence, clear eyesight and money
- Azurite: helps psychic powers, dreams and meditation
- Carnelian: dispels jealousy and anger, develops sexuality
- Citrine: for psychic awareness and creativity, dispels nightmares
- Haematite: for grounding, divination and intuition
- Jasper: for health, beauty and protection
- Lapis Lazuli: promotes healing, love, fidelity and psychic powers
- Moonstone: for divination, youth and Moon Magic
- Onyx: for protection and defensive Magic, helps control passions and emotions
- Tiger's-eye or Cat's-eye: attracts courage, luck and Earth energy
- Turquoise: attracts money, love, friends and healing
- Clear Quartz: magnifies psychic and healing energy; a power and protection crystal
- Smoky Quartz: overcomes depression and fatigue; empowering

Magic Moments, Seasons and Times

Connecting with the universal source of Magic has no time limits. It can be done at any second of the day and in any week of the year with great results, but there are certain Moon phases, seasons, and witching hours that can give an extra boost to your spellcasting and can help bring longer-lasting effects.

Moon Power

One of the most popular of the tried and true methods is to align a particular type of spell or ritual with the corresponding phase of the Moon. Even the most sceptic of scientists know that the Moon directly effects not only the Earth's tides, but also our most basic animal and human emotions. Many people are sensitive to the Moon's changing phases and all women of child-bearing age are both physically and emotionally effected through their own natural and 'lunar' based monthly cycles. Most witches keep a current Moon calendar handy (they can be purchased at New Age stores, or you can also look for a fishing guide in your local newsagent) so they can cast a close eye on the changing lunar cycles. The Moon orbits the

Earth in an anticlockwise 'widdershins' direction and has an approximate 28-day cycle as it grows or 'waxes' from the first day of the New Moon up to the Full Moon. It then goes into a diminishing or 'waning' phase back to begin the cycle all over again. Each of these different phases has a corresponding effect on your ritual.

⊚ Full Moon: for casting spells of love and high Magic
⊚ New Moon: to begin a new relationship or job
⊚ Waxing or Growing Moon: to attract growth, prosperity and commitment
⊚ Waning or Diminishing Moon: to finish a relationship or to banish negative energy

Lunar Cycles

There are 13 Full Moons (Esbats) in the year, and a Full Moon is a very powerful time for spellcasting and rituals.

The Harvest Moon is the Full Moon nearest the Autumn Equinox (Mabon).

'Once in a Blue Moon' happens in a year when a Full Moon appears twice in the same month.

Days of Enchantment

Another clever aid to spellcasting is to align your ritual with the corresponding day of the week. This can be very handy as a stopgap alignment where perhaps you want to cast a love spell or a prosperity charm, but due to time constraints, can't wait for a new or Full Moon to give it a mystical kick in the right direction. Each day of the week is ruled by at least one corresponding planet, so each particular day picks up the heavenly aspects of its very own guiding star.

◉ Sunday: Sun energy for casting spells of healing and tranquillity, and to invoke divine power

◉ Monday: Moon energy for beginnings, employment, clairvoyance and family

◉ Tuesday: Mars energy for debates, courage, physical strength and lust

◉ Wednesday: Mercury's influence for learning, teaching, predictions, self-improvement and communication

◉ Thursday: Jupiter power for wealth, legal matters, luck, materialism and expansion

◉ Friday: Venus energy for love, pleasure, art, music and partnerships

◉ Saturday: Saturn's influence for finalisation, departure and resolution

Sun Worship

Most people automatically associate the Moon and the stars with the old craft of Magic, but the Sun is actually the most ancient and constant symbol of wonder and enchantment and many of the sacred sites around the world were dedicated to either the Sun God or Goddess. Sunrise and midday are both perfect times to celebrate the precious life-giving solar rays and performing rituals at either times of the day can greatly enhance the power of certain spells.

Dawn Sun

The 'new born' sunrays at dawn have been revered since ancient times because the sunrise has always been considered sacred and an eternal miracle to behold. Sunrise can be a great time to enhance outdoor rituals or any kind of spells which incorporate new beginnings, abundance and fertility and power. The dawn of Midsummer Solstice is still considered the most powerful time of all, but for a modern witch any sunrise is just as awe inspiring and miraculous and can be used to empower many ceremonies and spellworking.

Midday Sun

As the Sun is at its peak it is another peak time for Magic and this hour has a double solar whammy because it's directly opposite to the Moon flavoured midnight and is backed up by the Magical power of the number 12.

My favourite spells to cast at midday are those that need a really big boost of life force, such as spells for getting over heartache and grief and also spells for prosperity and business dealings.

You can also dedicate a simple indoor or outdoor altar to the Sun by decorating a table with summertime flowers—especially sunflowers or yellow blooms—as well as seashells, aromatic potpourri and oranges and lemons.

Special colours associated with the Sun include white, red, corn yellow, and of course gold. Ritual candles can also include the colour blue to represent the sky in combination with yellow, red or gold.

The best crystals for Sun rituals include all green gemstones, especially emerald and jade as well as amber and yellow gems such as sapphires. Other powerful gemstones are tiger's-eye and lapiz lazuli. Spells should include the incenses of frankincense, sandalwood and ylang ylang, and for extra enchantment add the essential oils of saffron, lavender or clove to your oil burner. If you have your own herb garden, herbs gathered during the dawn or midday (particularly during midsummer) are extremely powerful and can be dried to use during the rest of the year.

To stimulate your creative ideas and imagination, create your own fantasy spells with pictures of enchanted animals associated with the Sun. Some favourites are sparrows and canaries, and mythical creatures like unicorns, firebirds, dragons and satyrs.

Leave a small mirror near your window for seven days to capture the light of the Sun. On the eighth day, sprinkle it with spring water and recite this self-dedication spell to attract success and happiness:

'O Goddess, I see you gaze through golden eyes;
so silently you speak your words.
A delicate stroll through crystal sands,
curling through perfumed corridors.
Now let this ancient alchemy awaken you,
let your sacred light come to me at last.'

91

Enchanted Seasons

The changing seasons bring different energies and we can perform ceremonies to help align us with the ebb and flow, the light and dark aspects of the natural universe and also to empower our spellworking. There are both contemporary rituals and old folklore ways to celebrate the seasons and for many witches, the magical Wheel of the Year influences not only our physical and spiritual connections to these cycles of climatic change, but also the eternal shape-shifting and merging of God and Goddess energies within nature and ourselves.

Symbolically, as the Wheel of the Year turns, the Great Mother Goddess gives birth to the Sun 'child' at Yule and as the magical Wheel keeps turning, the Triple Moon Goddess helps to purify the newborn energies and light up the night of Imbolc. Spring Equinox sees the developing of the young Sun God who is promised in marriage to the budding Maiden Goddess. As Beltane and Summer arrive and the Sun God fully matures into his physical form, he then appears on Earth as the powerful King Stag and makes passionate love to his fertile Goddess bride, the Queen Faery of the Flowers.

At Lugnasad comes the symbolic cutting of the mystical chord by the scythe of the Dark Sky Goddess, which also marks the last days of the Sun god's life in the earthly physical realm.

Then as the Autumn Equinox passes and the Old 'Hag' Goddess returns to cover the Earth in her Winter robe of ice and snow, the Sun god travels down into the realm of the spirits and underworld, where he becomes the Lord of the Hallows—only to be reborn as the Sun Child again at Yule through the nurturing belly, the eternal Magic cauldron of the Mother Goddess.

In the ancient pagan countryside, important fertility rites were performed during festival days to help balance the Earth's natural forces or to keep

the gods contented and happy. Even in today's urbanised world, many neo-pagans and witches follow as much as they can of the old ways.

The following festivals (also known as the Major Sabbats) date way back in time to the days of the ancient Celts, when Druid priests and priestesses were in charge of most religious and magical ceremonies.

◉ Samhain: One of the most ancient and biggest Celtic festivals marking the beginning of the old Druid year (which was originally based on a lunar calendar). A deeply spiritual and nocturnal time for long nights of hibernation and communing with the ancestors. Festivities often lasted the whole month of November.

◉ Imbolc: Post-Winter festival of the ancient Celts with purification ceremonies to reveal the first rays of sacred light and the blessing of the triple goddess, Brigid.

◉ Beltane: The other major festival for the Celts, the full re-awakening of the Earth and the return of daylight and the Sun god Bel. The virility of the natural world and the regenerating power of light were celebrated with bonfires and fertility and flower rites.

◉ Lugnasad: Honouring Lugh (the great warrior god of skills and knowledge) and the Mother Goddess (symbol of Ireland). A royal festival led by Lugh's earthly counterpart, the Celtic King, and celebrated with horse racing, dancing and poetry competitions.

Most other old Europeans, particularly the Germanic and Nordic people, enjoyed very similar kinds of festivals around the same days, but they also set aside extra days and rituals to mark the Winter and Summer Solstice as well as the Autumn and Spring Equinox. Throughout the ages and after constant invasions of the British Isles and Europe, there have been lots of mixing and blending between the Celtic, Gaelic and Germanic magical traditions and these four additional festivals (also called Minor Sabbats) are also celebrated by today's Wiccans as well as many other witches and neo-pagans.

@ Mabon: Autumn Equinox
@ Ostara: Spring Equinox
@ Yule: Midwinter Solstice
@ Litha: Midsummer Solstice

Southern Wheel of the Year

Not all covens or solitary witches perform rituals on all eight sabbats and there's no need to feel as if you must follow every single festival. Adaptations are always being made within the Craft—particularly in the Southern Hemisphere where the seasonal changes are not nearly so well-defined and the overall climate is so very different from that of Europe (not to mention the plants and animals). Whatever days you set aside for spiritual rituals or celebration should be your own choice and will depend very much on what kind of traditions you or your magical group relate to—and of course, what you can personally fit in with your family commitments and work schedule. Any of these sabbats and festival days can also be honoured beautifully and simply by having a celebratory meal with a few family members and friends, or just by lighting a candle and giving yourself a quiet moment alone for spiritual reflection and energy alignment.

Following is a list of festival days that has been adapted for the Southern Hemisphere, plus some tips on how they can be used to enhance both your meditation rituals and spellworking.

◎ Lugnasad (Lammas)

FEBRUARY 2

This was traditionally around the time of harvest, to celebrate the various skills and talents of the people. For us modern witches, it can be a time for emotional 'harvesting' as we take stock of our lives and remember not to take our own talents for granted—nor the blessings and abundance of the Earth. Take the time to really look on the bright side of life and spend some quality hours outdoors enjoying nature as much as you can, before the Autumn weather starts to set in. It is also a good time for defining what your talents are, writing down mission statements and casting prosperity spells.

◎ Mabon

MARCH 20 or 21
(AUTUMN EQUINOX)

This is a perfect time to start a saving program so that you can see what you can afford to put aside and store for the long Winter months ahead. Start being more careful not to waste time and being more discerning about what projects and problems to take on. The best rituals at this time are ones for creating balance and counting blessings. The night and day are of equal length, and this is a time of natural equilibrium, so you may use it to meditate and hone your visionary skills.

◎ Samhain (Halloween)

APRIL 30

In the Southern Hemisphere many witches celebrate Halloween on this
evening and it can be a great time for communing with Guardian
Angels and spirits, casting banishing spells and dispelling negative
vibes. In Germany this date is also 'Walpurgisnacht', a powerful and
mystical night when all the witches of the world come together and
dance around the fabled Brocken Mountain. (This night was and still
is my coven's New Year's celebration and has always proved to be a
special and sacred evening with Fenris and our inner circle.)

◎ Yule

JUNE 21 or 22
(MIDWINTER SOLSTICE)

In pagan times they celebrated the birth of the 'Sun Child' or 'Holly
King' during Yule. And you can also use this time to empower yourself
with the energy of rebirth and growth. This is the shortest day of the
year, where the Earth and the Sun appear to be stilled and suspended
together for a moment in time, so this a very magical day and
evening for rituals that can align you with the timeless aspects of the
eternal Universe. Spellworking can be enhanced by communing with
both your inner child and nurturing Mother Goddess energies.

◎ Imbolc (or Candelmas)

JULY 31

A great time for candle Magic for purification and celebrating the Moon. Also great for witchy initiations or re-affirming partnership vows. The Celtic traditions celebrated Brigid the Triple Goddess so you can also weave spells and rituals that incorporate Brigid or any of the Luna Goddess energies. Generally a good time for bringing some light into the shadowy or darker areas of your life and 'lightening up' by looking at the funny side of things, as well as pampering yourself with long baths or relaxing massages. Excellent too for house cleansingand banishing rituals with the sweeping of brooms both clockwisen and anticlockwise.

◎ Ostara

SEPTEMBER 21 or 22
(SPRING EQUINOX)

The light and dark energies are in perfect balance and this is the dawning of the solar festivals. The youthful Sun god and Maiden goddess energies are flowing through the Earth and rituals are best performed at daytime to take advantage of new possibilities, budding relationships and exciting projects. As well as reconnecting with the bloom of youthful vitality, perform any rituals that can help put a spring in your step and take full advantage of the potent vibrations around you.

◎ Beltane

OCTOBER 31

A lusty and joyous time with all the family and Magical
friends coming together in a full celebration of the love of life
as well as the blessing of procreation and fertility.
Great for marriage and handfasting rituals or baby naming
ceremonies. Also an excellent time for candle Magic,
casting Faery spells, along with boosting either physical or
spiritual fertility with abundance rituals and sex Magic.

◎ Litha

DECEMBER 21–22
(MID-SUMMER SOLSTICE)

The longest day of the year, traditionally a powerful time for solar
rituals and honouring the peak strength of the solar life force. Many
ancient temples and sacred sites were built with special altars and
archways that captured the Sun's Magical rays during the Summer
Solstice and this is a great time of the year to capture some of this
miraculous energy for yourself. Great for spells of empowerment,
growth and all forms of energising Magic.

essential witchery

spells, rituals and practical Magic

Get in touch with the witch within:
rites of awakening ~

rod and goddess power ~

Ye olde apothecary ~

Prosperity potions ~

Beauty and body charms ~

Love and sex charms ~

Dream weaver ~

Wikid ways ~

Kid power ~

Animal Magic ~

Broomstick travel ~

part *three*

Get in touch
with the
witch within:

rites of
awakening

Earthing Yourself

This ritual involving a tree can be used to align yourself with Earth—to feel grounded and to create the energy of that element in your life and spells, and to connect with the Magic of Earth itself.

You will need to gather:

◈ A long length of string (to be removed from tree after ritual)

Wrap and tie the string around the trunk of a large tree. Give it a big hug, then sit down on the ground with your back and spine aligned against the trunk and become conscious of the solidness of the ground beneath you. When you begin to feel yourself being pulled downwards and gaining strength and a solid foundation to your mind and body, repeat this incantation:

'Great Mother Earth, hold me in your arms of green and bring me close to your body of warmest brown. I join with the strength and rhythm of your deepest eternal heart. So Mote It Be.'

High as a Kite

Take advantage of lovely breezes and windy weather to align with the magical element of Air.

You will need to gather:

🌀 *a length of blue material or ribbon*

On a breezy day, tie one end of the fabric or ribbon to a fence, a tree branch or a clothesline. Then, stand and watch the ribbon fly and wave in the wind. While consciously feeling the breeze, say these words out loud:

> 'Now blow you winds from North and South,
> warm then cold from East to West,
> spin and turn, fly and flow,
> whisper charms wherefore you go.'

Leave the ribbon in place for as long as you like. You can also add more for family and friends to enjoy.

Become One With Water

Sit near a lake, swim in the ocean or walk in a light rain as a first step to working with the magical natural element of Water.

Then call on Manannan mac Lir, a sea god and, in the old Celtic world, a Master of Magic. He is also known as the 'Lord of Mists' and 'Lord of the Land Beneath the Waves'. Think of his strength and call his name when you want to invoke a strong sense of the ocean and the mystical seas.

'Hail to you Manannan mac Lir, Lord of the Mists, Lord of the Waves—
I feel your strength from between the Ways,
In the eye of the storm, your heart beats like a drum
From the salty depths of the Sea we rise up now—together as one!'

Feel the Fire
Element of Fire

Whenever you are lucky enough to sit by an open fire really take the time to absorb the energy, breathe in the wonderful smell of the burning wood and think about what an amazing gift it is. For an easy connection with the element of fire, simply light a candle and sit nearby while gazing at the centre of the flame. Without coming too close or blowing out the flame, wave your hand near the candle and feel the warmth and observe how the flame moves and dances around. Then just sit quietly a short distance away and really focus your mind on the flame and see whether you can 'will' the candle flame to move up and down or right and left or spin around just by thinking about it. To help you focus on this part of the ritual, say this incantation a few times:

'Sacred flame, do as I say,
Sacred flame, dance and play.'

When you feel energised and ready to end the ritual, say these words:

'Sacred flame, do as I will,
Sacred flame, now be still.'

And then blow out the flame completely.

Cosmic Awakener and Self-initiation

Two of the most treasured and valuable lessons I've learnt through my own journey is that we are all connected to the eternal source of Magic and that every spiritual path in the world holds symbolic keys to cosmic truth and meaning. We are all part of an ancient, Universal Tradition.

This ritual helps awaken you to the boundless source of cosmic knowledge and can also be used as a self-initiation into Universal Magic.

Spend time meditating on each of the symbols written below; you can even copy or trace them out on a piece of paper if you wish. Focus for at least seven minutes on each symbol until you've concentrated on all of them, and do this once a day, in either the morning or the evening, for no less than 21 days.

Symbols are the Celtic cross, the ankh, the star of David, the yin and yang symbol, the witch's star pentacle, the eye of Horus, the infinity symbol and the spiral.

After you have performed this 21-day ritual, look into a mirror and say:

'I am a magical and eternal being and the Universe and I awaken the witch within.'

Past-life Vision Booster

To help you get a clearer view of past lives, cast this spell on the day of a New Moon and repeat it once every week for a month.

Take a small white onion and soak it in a bowl of mineral water for half an hour and then take it out and dry it thoroughly with a clean cloth. Meditate for a few minutes while you hold the onion in your hands and then start to peel off the first and second layers of the onion while you repeat this incantation:

'Memories of the distant past, come forward into the light.'

Place the layers you have peeled off into a paper bag and bury near a tree. Keep the rest of the onion wrapped in the refrigerator to use again.

Don't just believe it can happen, know it and see that it already has.

God and Goddess Power

Lift the veil of superstition when you talk to the gods and goddesses. Losing yourself to fear or superstition is magically disempowering. We can still commune and feel at one with all the inspirational magic of the ancient gods and goddesses without bowing down or feeling less worthy than they are.

There's also no need to look at the god/dess energies as if they are completely separate from you, because that is a psychological 'giving up' of your personal power.

Knowing you are responsible for your own thoughts and actions is magically empowering. A real witch is a lead player in her own game of life.

You are just as much a part of the cosmic order as are the god and goddess energies. Summoning the ancient gods and goddesses is a summoning up of the natural forces and the different personas within yourself, which helps connect you with the myriad of archetypal energies throughout the universe.

As my good friend and sister witch Leonora says: 'There is quite a difference between praying to a great goddess and just saying "please help me", and saying, "Dear Great Goddess, I am you and you are me".

'Saying it without arrogance and knowing that you not only communicate with and are a part of the gods, you *are* the goddess and gods, you *are* the rain, you *are* the earth, the sky, you are that big, that all-knowing.

'And even if that realisation, that knowing, is just for a split second during ritual or while simply meditating and connecting to your Magic, that's okay, because that is true Magic—knowing you are All That Is.'

I've chosen some of my favourite god/dess spells to remind you that every one of us can be empowered by our inner Magic. With the right incantation, you can also call on whatever type of god/dess nature you need to inspire and balance your life.

The Warrior

When you need to use your warrior energy and assertive nature (this can be a god or goddess ritual), rise early on a Monday morning and cast this spell before you begin your daily routine.

Take a refreshing shower using an aloe body gel and a firm sponge or loofah to slough off any dull and dry skin from your body.

Stand under the warm water while you wash away all of your timid energy and shyness. Feel yourself being filled with new vigour and energy.

When you feel refreshed, wrap yourself in a large towel and look into your bathroom mirror as you say:

> 'I am the Warrior, I recognise my eternal strength.
> There's nothing I cannot achieve, no road I cannot travel,
> no barriers to my success.
> I am woman (man) full of power.'

Young God/dess

Recognise and have fun with your inner child by casting this spell at any time you need an energy lift.

You will need to gather:

- ❀ gold glitter
- ❀ glue
- ❀ a pair of your old shoes

Place all your spell ingredients on a flat surface and coat the outside of your shoes with glue.

Sprinkle the gold glitter evenly over the gluey shoes, covering as much of the surface area you can. Leave to dry completely.

When the shoes are dry to touch, stand in front of a full-length mirror in your home and slip into the shoes. Then click your heels together three times, look into the mirror and say:

> 'Hello again, young child, let's come out to play.
> We'll have fun and joy forever more
> and inside me you'll always stay.'

Put on your Magic shoes whenever you need a boost of happiness.

The Nurturing God/dess

All women (and men) can enjoy their independent natures and at the same time still connect with their nurturing and maternal instincts. To honour your inner Earth Mother energy, cast this spell on a Sunday afternoon.

You will need to gather:

- an egg
- a piece of wholemeal bread
- a trowel or spade

Go outside to a safe place in either your backyard or a park and sit down on the ground with your spell items around you.

Hold the egg and bread in your hands while you breathe deeply and focus on your gentle and maternal nature. Then say:

'From Mother Nature we are all born,
nurturing, protective and giver of life.
I now connect with my nurture energy, O Blessed Be.'

Next, dig a hole in the ground and bury the egg and bread in the earth.

The Mystic God/dess

We often forget to look after our spiritual and psychic nature, and this spell can help align you with the cosmic energies around you.

You will need to gather:

- a clear quartz crystal
- red henna powder or non-toxic red water-based paint
- a small paintbrush

Find some time to be alone and undisturbed for at least half an hour, and dress in some comfortable, light-coloured clothing.

Using the paintbrush, apply a small red dot to your third eye chakra (on your forehead) and also paint a dot on the palm of each of your hands.

Sit cross-legged on the floor while you hold the crystal in your two hands and breathe calmly and deeply while you meditate and let go of thoughts of daily stresses and worries.

Next, repeat this incantation:

'Thank you, oh universe,
for my awareness of the eternal power of spirit.
I open my psychic mind to the Mystic Goddess.'

The Wise Wo/man

Our experiences and ups and downs in life make us wiser and more able to make tough decisions. To help honour our growing maturity and wisdom, cast this spell on any day of the week.

You will need to gather:

- 1 cup of salt
- a handful of cloves

Go to a quiet place in your home.

Stand in the centre of the room and sprinkle the salt in a clockwise circle around you.

Then sprinkle the cloves in a clockwise direction around you. Stand in the middle of this circle, with your arms in the air, as you repeat this incantation:

'Spirit of the North, grant me knowledge
    and tolerance,
blessed be the wo/man within me
who brings wisdom and understanding.'

Seal the spell's power by scooping up the salt and cloves from the floor and keep the mixture in a small wooden or cardboard box.

Ye Olde Apothecary
Setting Up Your Enchanted Kitchen

In centuries past, both the country and town folk would ask their village 'witch doctor' to cook them up a healing brew in times of illness, or a potion to fire up their fertility or chances for romance. These old wise people were really the original medicos. Going back as far in history as ancient Europe, Asia and Egypt (and let's not forget the African and Australian continents), they understood the healing power of herbs and insect and animal products. Certain cultures used a specially brewed beer (an original form of tetracycline), mouldy bread (penicillin), snake, toad and spider venoms (anti-disease and anti-cancer properties).

Along with being clever herbalists, many of these witchy medicos were also adept clairvoyants and psychics. They spent many of their days (and, of course, nights) brewing up spellbinding goodies over their bubbling cauldrons and enchanted kitchen fires.

You'll most probably want to skip the snake and wiggly spider bits (handling disagreeable toads is a favourite pastime of mine, but that's another story). There's plenty of scope for you to brew up delicious and magically healing recipes, using safe and palatable ingredients.

I like to write my recipes either in a computer file or an old school exercise book that I've had for years and I still call both systems 'Ye Olde Cookery Book'.

You don't have to go overboard with your 'enchanted kitchen'. If space is a problem you can make one like mine, which is really about making a specific area in a kitchen or laundry cupboard where you can store your witchy ingredients. As long as they're properly tagged, you can store herbs and things in well-washed coffee or jam jars on your kitchen bench. You

could also have a lot of fun with it and make a really 'witchy feature' in your kitchen where you can hang a straw broom and pretty dried flowers, and grow fresh herbs in small pots.

Magic Kitchen Basics

When you first begin to create your own spells and rituals, you might like to put together your own basic spell kit. This could include:

- A mortar and pestle (preferably stone or metal) for grinding and mixing herbs and spices.
- A variety of glass containers, such as well-washed coffee or jam jars, for storing ingredients and potions.
- A small metal tea-ball for brewing single cups of herbal teas and tonics.
- Pieces of cheesecloth, which are useful for straining brews and for making sachets.
- A tea kettle and a china or metal teapot for magical infusions.
- A cauldron is optional; you can still stir up beautiful Magic with a selection of modern pots and pans.

Ingredients and Saucery— Almonds

- **Esoteric Magic**—has an erotic and arousing vibration and is also used in love and fertility spells.
- **Practical Magic**—healing and beauty treatments. Famed for their beautiful flavour and wonderful healing powers in ancient Greece and Rome, the oil, meal and milk of almonds were used in tonics, breads and skin creams well before Christian times.

Hands of Aphrodite

For smooth and blemish-free hands and arms, mix together this ancient recipe on either a Friday (the day of Venus or Aphrodite) or during a waning, diminishing moon.

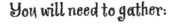

You will need to gather:

- 150 grams of raisins or sultanas
- 150 grams of blanched almonds (unsalted and peeled)
- 1 teaspoon of lemon juice
- half a cup of full cream milk (not skim)
- approx half a cup of flat beer (any type will do)

First put the raisins and the blanched almonds into your mortar dish and grind them with your pestle (you can use an electric blender if you prefer). Then add the lemon juice and slowly add the milk. Mix well with a wooden spoon. Next, drip in the beer a little bit at a time, just enough until you have a nice, thick paste.

Then before you take your next shower or bath, wipe the mixture over the back of your hands and over your arms (you can even put it over your entire body if you wish) and leave it on for at least 15 minutes, and then wash it off thoroughly in your shower.

Throw away the remaining mixture and just make a fresh batch the next time you give yourself the 'Aphrodite' treatment.

Aloe Vera

- **Esoteric Magic**—has a peaceful and cleansing vibration, and can be used in protection and healing spells.

- **Practical Magic**—an essential healing plant for just about everything. Every witch should have an aloe vera plant growing in a pot or her garden and they are very easy to maintain indoors or outdoors. It also soothes sunburnt skin and heals scars.

Vera Vitality

This healing drink is best freshly made in the morning and drunk before you get on with the day's activities. It helps cleanse the kidneys and liver, and will give you extra vitality.

You will need to gather:

- *aloe vera gel (break off a small piece of your aloe vera plant and scoop out the inside gel with a spoon—don't eat the skin)*
- *some of your favourite fruit or vegetable juice*

Before you eat your breakfast, pour out a small or medium glass of juice. Squeeze in the aloe vera gel and stir briskly with a long spoon and drink at your leisure.

Apples

- **Esoteric Magic**—the magic symbol for love and fertility. The emblem of Aphrodite or Venus. One of the sacred Druid trees.

- **Practical Magic**—an apple a day keeps the doctor away, as well as being a natural teeth cleaner. Apple juice is a blood cleanser and is packed full of vitamins.

Apple Water

This old recipe is for a healing drink for fevers and hot flushes.

You will need to gather:

- *3 – 4 apples, unpeeled*
- *1 litre of water*
- *a little sugar*

Slice the apples thinly, cover with the water in a saucepan, add the sugar and simmer until the apple slices become soft.

Strain the liquid and allow to cool to room temperature. Throw away the apple slices and drink the liquid either warm or ice cold.

Blackberries

- **Esoteric Magic**—robust and lively vibrations used for both health and romantic spells and potions.

- **Practical Magic**—a favourite of the ancient Europeans; both the fruit and juice were used for medicinal purposes.

Blackberry Booster

Blackberries have been used for centuries by spellcasters to energise the body. You can use this recipe to make a healing drink or an external compress (see below).

You will need to gather:

- 1 cup of fresh blackberries
- a few cloves
- 1 – 2 tablespoons of sugar or honey
- a glass jar with a lid
- mineral or spring water (or brandy)

Press the juice out of the blackberries, and add the cloves and sugar or honey. Heat in a saucepan and simmer until the mixture becomes syrupy. Allow it to cool and store in the glass jar.

To make a refreshing magical drink, add a spoonful to a glass of mineral or spring water, or heat some syrup and drink it warm with a nip of brandy.

Chamomile

- **Esoteric Magic**—chamomile's vibrations are peaceful and curative, and it is used for meditative and healing spells.
- **Practical Magic**—an ancient remedy for nausea and mental stress. One of the nine sacred herbs of the Saxons, who called it 'maythen', chamomile can also be grown near sick plants to improve their health. It can be drunk as a tea, and also can be used in skincare products and hair care.

Coriander

- **Esoteric Magic**—increases hypnotic vibrations and is used for tranquillity and psychic spells.
- **Practical Magic**—pieces of coriander were found carefully wrapped in the tomb of the Egyptian Pharaoh Rameses. Used for thousands of years in medicine and for magical foods and sauces.

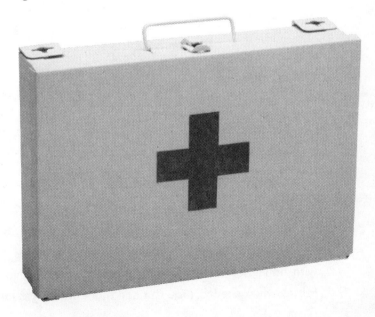

Garlic

- **Esoteric Magic**—protective and purifying resonance; its vibrations are steeped in occult history. Necklaces can be made from stringing together fresh or dried bulbs and hung up around the kitchen for good luck. It can also be used for banishing and protective spells.

- **Practical Magic**—highly esteemed by both old and new witchy doctors and used for thousands of years as a food and medicine. One of the first known antibacterial agents since ancient times. Eases sore throats, colds and flu and helps to lower high blood pressure and cholesterol levels. The fresh garlic bulb contains the best healing properties and is much better than the tablets.

Kickagermjoy Juice

Try this amazing healing potion for cleansing the liver and blood. It is especially good for helping to clear up a bad flu and also chest colds.

- 3 or 4 whole garlic bulbs
- 5 lemons
- honey to taste
- 8 cups of water
- 1 ginger root

Peel and roughly chop up all of the garlic bulbs and put them into a large saucepan. Pour in the eight glasses of water.

Chop up the lemons and ginger and also put into the saucepan.

Bring the water to the boil and simmer on low for 5 minutes. Turn off the heat and let it sit for another 10 minutes, then strain off the liquid into another saucepan or a jug and throw away the leftover solids. Drink a cup of the liquid with honey for taste and keep the rest in the fridge for up to two days and reheat when needed. (You can add more water if it tastes too strong for you.)

Magic is real and dreams can come true.

Ginger

- **Esoteric Magic**—uplifting and passionate vibrations for prosperity and love potions

- **Practical Magic**—used for thousands of years in Asian medicine. Antibacterial and good for colds and clearing sinuses, and to relieve mild constipation. Adds zip and zing to any dish, especially fish and chicken dishes.

Goat's Milk and Yoghurt

- **Esoteric Magic**—cleansing and beautifying resonance, used in love and sex potions and beauty spells.

- **Practical Magic**—the original glamour queens of Babylon and ancient Egypt swore by the beautifying power of goat's milk, and interestingly enough it has now been scientifically proven to contain alpha-hydroxy agents as well the best kind of healing bacteria. Cleo and the rest of the ancient Divas drank and bathed in goat's milk products, and so should any 'glamour-savvy' witch.

Pour half a bottle of goat's milk into your bath along with a dash of lavender for soft, healthy skin; mix the other half of the bottle with some fresh strawberries or bananas for a power-packed breakfast drink.

Honey

- **Esoteric Magic**—resonance of passion and love, used in witchery for fertility, romance and marriage spells.

- **Practical Magic**—a fantastic all-round health food and source of vitamins. Used in ancient Europe and Egypt in food and drink and to soothe burns and dry skin.

Honey and Roses

You will need to gather:

- *a tub of natural honey*
- *1 cup of fresh rose petals (any colour, but red is the strongest)*
- *3 cups of water*

Boil the rose petals in the water. Simmer for five minutes and then turn off the heat and leave to stand for 10 minutes. Strain the rose water into a jug, and throw away the petals. Mix the honey into the rose water and store in an airtight container in the fridge, where it will keep for at least a month or so. It can be used for sore throats or mouth ulcers by simply adding a few teaspoons of the honey rose mixture to herbal tea as a healthy and enchanting drink.

Horseradish

- **Esoteric Magic**—strong protective vibrations and cleansing resonance. Used for banishing spells.
- **Practical Magic**—since olden times, used as a remedy for digestive problems. It was also wrapped into warm cloths and put around limbs and joints to relieve mild rheumatism.

Remedial Recipe

You will need to gather:

- 1 teaspoon of horseradish
- 1 teaspoon of dry, mild mustard (French mustard is good)
- 1 cup of apple-cider vinegar
- 2 cups of water
- 3 long pieces of cheesecloth

Mix the horseradish, mustard, vinegar and water together in a saucepan. Heat the mixture on the stove for 5 minutes.

Next, turn off the heat and allow the mixture to stand until it reaches room temperature. Then dip in one of the lengths of cheesecloth and wrap it around your aching joint (make sure there are no scratches or open wounds around the joint or it could sting a bit).

Then follow with the next two layers of dry cheesecloth and leave on for at least 20 minutes.

Lemons and Limes

- **Esoteric Magic**—uplifting and cleansing vibration, to enhance renewal. Used in energising spells and banishing rituals.

- **Practical Magic**—relieves colds, sore throats and fever, warts, insect bites and greasy skin. A fantastic source of vitamin C and used in many magical foods and healing drinks.

Lemon Lift

Make this delicious and uplifting tea which helps reduce fever during flu or chest colds.

You will need to gather:

- 1 lemon or 2 limes
- 1 teaspoon of raspberry jam
- 1 teaspoon of honey (optional)
- 1 or 2 fresh mint leaves (optional)
- 1 cup of hot water

Squeeze the lemon or limes, and pour the juice into the bottom of a cup. Stir in the jam and honey (to taste), then pour in the hot water to fill the rest of the cup. Add the mint leaves if you wish and then drink at any time of the day or especially before bed if you have a cold.

Lemon Balm

- **Esoteric Magic**—soothing and calming vibrations. Used for family and home protection spells.

- **Practical Magic**—has been used since time immemorial as a wound dressing. It also makes a nice-tasting and mildly sedative tea to help you sleep. You can purchase tea bags or loose tea and pour on hot water with honey or raw sugar for taste before bedtime for a restful night's sleep.

Mint

- **Esoteric Magic**—activating and clearing vibrations. Used for focus and concentration spells and for success rituals.

- **Practical Magic**—the herb can be grown easily in pots and is a must-have addition to any witch's kitchen. Is an all-round additive for pick-me-up drinks and meals. When eaten regularly, it can help relieve nausea and headaches. Wonderful on its own or as an addition to any hot or cold herbal tea.

Witch's Brew

You will need to gather:

- *a slice of lemon*
- *1 teaspoon of orange marmalade*
- *2 cups of hot water*
- *1 teaspoon of fresh mint or mint tea*
- *1 teaspoon of chamomile tea*

Place all the ingredients in a teapot and pour in the hot water. Allow the brew to sit for 5 minutes as you repeat this incantation:

'Earth, Fire, Air and Sea,
Natural Magic come to me.'

Nutmeg

- **Esoteric Magic**—stimulating vibration. Used for casting money and success spells.
- **Practical Magic**—ancient medicinal qualities for poor circulation and exhaustion. Go easy on how much you sprinkle onto food, as it too much can be slightly hallucinogenic—which is exactly why it was often used in 'flying' formulas.

To make your own mild flying formula to give you a kick start for a successful day ahead, sprinkle a small amount into a yoghurt milkshake and drink it early in the day. Take some nutmeg with you to work and sprinkle a little pinch of it around you in the afternoon before a big meeting.

Onions

- **Esoteric Magic**—highly protective and purifying vibrations, used in banishing spells and looking into the past.
- **Practical Magic**—the use of this plant is so ancient that it is said Hippocrates, the father of medicine, recommended onion juice as a curative for just about everything. Don't go so far as drinking the juice, but definitely try and use onions in lots of your cooking because it is a great blood cleanser, helps relieve water retention and aids the lymphatic system.

Oranges

- **Esoteric Magic**—uplifting vibrations. Ruled by the power of the Sun, used in love, healing and pregnancy spells.
- **Practical Magic**—Strengthens the heart and another great source of vitamin C.

Squeeze fresh orange juice at least once or twice a week for you and your family for a powerful dose of Sun power. To help stimulate fertile power, roll an orange softly over your tummy.

Parsley

🌀 **Esoteric Magic** —stimulating and healing vibrations. Used for protection and family spells.

🌀 **Practical Magic** —high in vitamins A and C, it has been used for centuries in the treatment of kidney and bladder problems as well as sciatica. It is said that parsley also helps to relieve labour pains, and it can be chewed after meals to freshen the breath.

Pepper (Black and White)

🌀 **Esoteric Magic**—banishing and cleansing vibrations. Used for both hexing and healing spells.

🌀 **Practical Magic**—used for over 3,000 years in India and China as a food and in medicine as a treatment for heartburn, stiff muscles and colic.

Sprinkle it over food to stimulate appetite and to add zest and power to any savoury dish.

Rosehips

- **Esoteric Magic**—arousing and healing vibrations. Used in love potions and also wonderful for Faery spells and rituals.

- **Practical Magic**—the oil helps to heal scars and is a wonderful addition to skin cream. It can be purchased as a herbal tea and is a lovely healing drink for monthly cramps.

Faery Basket

Place baskets of rosehips and geranium and lavender potpourri around your home to attract Faery Magic and to have insightful dreams.

Rosemary

- **Esoteric Magic**—probably one of the most important witchy plants (most old folk charmers would have a rosemary bush growing outside to protect the home). With high Magic and protective resonance, and good for just about every kind of spell, it adds power to most rituals.

- **Practical Magic**—rosemary is an aid to digestion, clears the blood and liver and is a wonderful addition to hair and skin tonics. Always have a bunch hanging somewhere in the magical kitchen for both good luck and good health.

Roses

- **Esoteric Magic**—arousing and passionate vibrations. Also has a sacred 'goddess' resonance. It was once the custom to suspend a rose over a conference or dinner table to bring truth and sacred energy to the

conversation (hence the still-used 'ceiling rose'); also great for love and sexuality spells.

◉ **Practical Magic**—a blood cleanser and natural antiseptic agent with a wonderfully pleasant flavour. Used for centuries in food and medicines.

Rose-Petal Butter

You will need to gather:

◉ *1 cup of fresh red rose petals*
◉ *a glass jar with a lid*
◉ *125 grams of butter wrapped in waxed paper*
◉ *a few slices of white bread*

Sprinkle a layer of rose petals into the bottom of the jar, then put in the butter wrapped in waxed paper. Cover again with another layer of rose petals. Twist the lid of the jar on firmly and leave in the fridge or a cool room overnight. The stronger the scent of the roses, the better the flavour of the butter will be.

The next day, cut up some fresh white bread into finger-sized pieces or triangles, and spread generously with the scented butter as well as sprinkling more fresh petals between the slices and over the dish.

Salt

- Esoteric Magic—the use of salt in Magic goes way back to antiquity. Cleansing, protective and with high Magic resonance, it is used for clearing and banishing spells and to prepare altars and areas for all kinds of sorcery. A must-have in any witchy kitchen.

- Practical Magic—used in the olden days as a cleanser and antibiotic agent, still great in warm water as a gargle for sore throats and toothache. Adds taste to foods but go easy as it does help to retain water.

Bless This House

Mix a pinch of rosemary and salt together in a bowl and stand in the Magical hearth (the kitchen) of your home and walk in a widdershins (anti-clockwise) direction just once around the room, sprinkling the mixture as you go.

Next, stand in the kitchen and relax your body and mind. Visualise the circle of salt mixture now expanding and growing outwards so that your whole house or apartment is now encircled with cleansing energy.

After a moment or two, get your broom (preferably straw, of course!) and sweep up the mixture into a dustpan.

The very moment you awaken your search for Magical knowledge is the moment you consciously become a magician.

Prosperity Potions
Good Luck and Money Oil

Money and lottery spells will work best if you have lots of fun casting them, and then relax and let the universe take its course.

You will need to gather:

- ten-dollar note
- an eyedropper
- a clear quartz crystal
- peppermint essential oil
- lemongrass essential oil
- 1 small bottle of almond oil

On a Wednesday or the night of a New Moon, place the ten-dollar note onto a clean table and then place the clear quartz crystal on top. Put the rest of your spell items nearby on the table and then, with an eye dropper, put three drops each of the peppermint and lemongrass essential oils into the bottle of almond oil. Firmly screw the lid back onto the almond oil and start shaking the bottle quite vigorously as you say:

> 'Shake up, shake up spirits of money and wealth,
> take out, take out bad luck and now bring me success instead.'

Next, put the bottle back on the table, unscrew the lid and wipe a drop of the Magic oil onto the ten-dollar note as well as a drop or two over the quartz crystal. Leave them overnight to be charged by the power of the Moon.

In the morning, put the ten-dollar note back into your wallet and keep the ey oil in a cool place to be used whenever you need to attract good fortune.

Problem Solver

To make the correct decision concerning a problem, burn a mixture of sandalwood and frankincense essential oils in an oil burner and meditate until the right way forward is revealed to you.

Smell the Roses

Sprinkle your clothing with rosewater for a good day and good feelings.

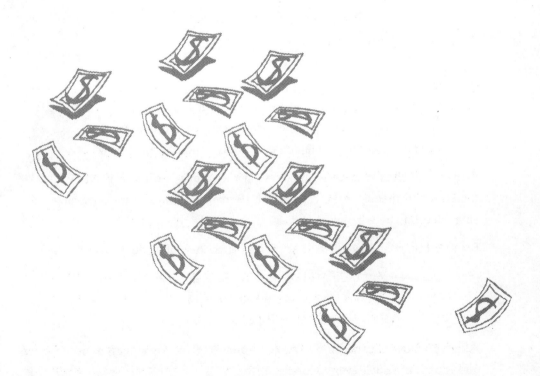

Lottery Luck

Use this spell to bring prosperity and good fortune in the lottery. But keep in mind my Good Witch's rule for money Magic: 'Only gamble with money you can afford to lose.' In other words, lucky charms can only work if you just spend spare change and never dip into your savings.

You will need to gather:

- a green cloth
- a pyrite stone (available at crystal shops)
- a green candle
- a white candle holder
- 3 almonds
- a small bowl
- a sheet of clean white paper

On a Monday evening, create a lucky altar in your living room by laying the cloth on a side table and then placing on top the pyrite stone, the candle in the candle holder and the almonds in the bowl.

Write your chosen lottery numbers on the paper and place it into the bowl and then light the candle. For 10 minutes concentrate on seeing yourself with the winning ticket.

Breathe calmly and evenly and hold the pyrite in your hand as you say:

> 'Mother Earth, Father Fire,
> bring me what I desire.
> So Mote It Be.'

After you blow out the candle, leave the altar in place for at least a month or so and repeat the spell every Monday.

Winning Numbers

Invoke the power of lucky Jupiter to help you pick some winning numbers.

You will need to gather:

- peppermint incense
- a sheet of white paper
- a small piece of putty or Blu-Tac
- green paint or a green marking pen
- a 30-cm length of red cord
- two small pebbles
- 1 teaspoon of sage
- a sheet of red paper

One week before you buy your lottery ticket, light the incense and place the piece of white paper on a table along with the Blu-Tac and green paint or marker and cord, and sit comfortably nearby. Pick up the putty or Blu-Tac and roll it into a ball with your hands. Then press it with your left thumb and put a dab of green paint or pen on the thumbprint. Wrap up the ball with the red cord and while you hold it carefully, repeat these words:

'With the Seal of Jupiter,
by the power of Mercury,
give me numbers on a count of three.'

Put down the ball and clap your hands three times and then write down the first numbers that come into your mind. Repeat the chant until you have as many numbers as you need, and leave the Magic ball near your money documents.

After you have purchased your lottery ticket, place it between the two pebbles. Then stand about a metre away with the sage in your right hand. Look towards the pebbles and sprinkle the sage in a clockwise direction around you as you repeat this incantation:

> 'Aradia, Fortuna, carry your winning way
> towards me from this day.'

Finish the spell by wrapping up your lottery ticket in the red paper and saying:

> 'It Will Be So.'

This spell takes some time and patience but works like a charm to help you pick your Magic numbers.

The Luck of the Irish

An enchanting tradition for attracting luck with money is to make a cup of chamomile tea, allow it to cool completely and then place it in the refrigerator for an hour.

Wash your hands in the cold chamomile tea and wipe your hands with a clean towel as you say:

> 'With the luck of the Shamrock,
> from times of old,
> allow my path
> to be paved with gold.'

For Good Fortune Faeries

Attract the Faeries of luck into your house by wiping down your front and back door with a white cloth that has been soaked in a mixture of 2 cups of spring water and 3 drops of tea-tree oil.

Wonderstones

The ancient Druids wore enchanted Adder Stones on their fingers or as a pendant to bring good luck and health. Adder Stones are made from a ring-shaped crystal or a stone with a natural hole in the middle.

For a powerful protection charm, find a piece of amber that contains some fossilised insects and keep it near your front door.

If you don't want to go to the expense of purchasing a special stone, keep your eye out for any oddly shaped or appealing pebbles on the ground, and keep the stone you choose in a drawstring bag as your own mystical 'Wonderstone'. (To ensure its lasting power, don't let anyone else touch it.)

Attracting Abundance

Have you ever heard of the affirmation, 'Money will come when I'm ready to receive it'? This spell will get you into a winning state of mind.

You will need to gather:

- a silver candle
- some nutmeg
- a few cloves
- a small bowl

On the night of a New or Growing Moon, light the candle and mix the nutmeg and cloves in the bowl.

As you feel yourself surrounded by positive thoughts and energy, repeat these Magic words:

> 'Artemis, Darius, call abundance to my vicinity.
> Summon the call of prosperity,
> as is my right, O Blessed Be.'

Blow out the candle after 20 minutes and bury the nutmeg and cloves near your front door.

New Year Magic

Instead of making the same old New Year resolutions, why not cast a lucky New Year spell instead.

As well as for the New Year, you can cast this spell on the ninth of any month at nine o'clock in the morning or night.

Light a gold candle and sit comfortably nearby while you relax your mind and body for a few moments. On a piece of purple paper, write down your wishes for the New Year nine times, then repeat these words:

> 'Copper, gold, silver, tin,
> as the year proceeds, my luck is in.'

Keep your wish list in a special place and make sure you read it regularly.

The Good Oil

To rid yourself of negative energy and bad luck, take a framed photo of yourself, place it face upward, and rub coconut oil over it.

The study of Magic will allow you to open up all the possibilities of the universe, and encourage your own human and spiritual development.

Beauty and Body Charms

Society puts a lot of emphasis on health and looks nowadays, and even though men and women come in a wonderful variety of beautifully natural shapes and sizes which are perfectly normal and healthy for them, many people feel stressed and pressured about their body image, or feel as if they need to lose weight really fast.

Of course, there is no Magic spell that is going to make you lose weight overnight so that ZAP! you are suddenly a famous supermodel. But I do believe that true beauty and a good self-image do come from within and Magic can help with rituals to relax you and help you to learn to love yourself. Be proud and happy with whatever body the wonderful universe is lending you while you are here in this dimension, and enjoy this wonderful planet we call Mother Earth.

To follow are a few self-esteem and healthy body spells to have fun with and to help to de-stress and maintain the greatest magical temple of all—your own god/dess-given body!

Dear Diary

Start up an enchanted diary by finding a new notebook and writing on the cover, 'My Wonderful Life'. Each day, write down at least one positive thing that happened to you during the day. It can be anything that makes you feel good, such as 'I saw a gorgeous sunset' or 'I had a productive day at work' or 'A young child smiled at me.' Read through the pages each week to keep yourself inspired and motivated.

Mirror Mirror

True beauty starts from within and radiates outwards to give you charisma and confidence.

Find some time for yourself when you can be alone for a while, and take a relaxing warm shower or bath. After you have patted yourself dry, remain skyclad (the magical term for being naked) and stand in front of your bathroom mirror. Place a lightly scented body lotion nearby and start looking at your own reflection in the mirror, starting with your face, concentrating especially on your eyes. As you look into your eyes, repeat this incantation:

> 'Inside me beautiful Magic lives,
> my eyes are windows to an enchanted place.'

Next, smile a big smile and let yourself have a giggle or a laugh if you feel like it. Then put your hands softly up to touch your face and repeat this incantation:

> 'Inside me wonderful Magic lives,
> I can feel its glow when I touch my face.'

Then, squeeze some of the lotion onto your palms and rub it gently over your entire body, feeling yourself being filled with positive energy and power. When you are ready to get dressed, seal the spell's Magic with these words:

> 'I will honour myself and my glorious mind, spirit and body.'

Superbody

Cook up this enchanted brew to help you curb your appetite for junk food.

You will need to gather:

- 2 carrots
- 3 tomatoes
- a small bunch of celery
- 1 sprig of parsley
- 3 cups of spring water
- 1 sprig each of thyme and marjoram

Wash the vegetables and parsley well, then chop them up and place them in a saucepan with the spring water. Simmer for 10 minutes or until soft. Stir with a wooden spoon and sprinkle in the thyme and marjoram as you repeat this incantation:

'Here is energy and joy anew.
Inspiring forces are in this brew.'

Allow the soup to cool, then strain the liquid into a bowl. As you throw the cooked vegetables into the garbage bin, say:

'There go my old worries and woe.'

Drink a cup of the Magic liquid before lunch or dinner. It can be stored in the refrigerator for just a day or two, then discard and make a fresh batch.

Good Habits

This spell works like a charm to get rid of any habits like smoking or niggling worries.

You will need to gather:

- *a cup*
- *a white candle*
- *sandalwood incense*

Set the empty cup on a table in front of the candle. Light the incense and the candle, and stand near the table as you pick up the cup in both hands and hold it high over the candle and incense.

Breathe slowly and evenly for a moment until you are calm and centred.

Then, hold the cup near your chest and slowly blow air into it, silently naming each bad habit and negative energy you wish removed from your life. When finished, turn the cup upside down onto the table, saying firmly:

'The contents of this vessel, I give up to thee,
Lords of Light,
exchange these bad habits for positive actions.'

Finish by blowing out the candle and incense and saying:

'It shall be done, O Blessed Be.'

The Time Is Right

One of the most magical times to begin a new health regime is at the beginning of a Waning or Diminishing Moon (when the Moon is moving from full back to new). This will give a special boost to your bid for a fitter and healthier body.

Lunar Locks

To help your hair grow long and lustrous, only trim it on a day or evening of a Full Moon.

Shiny Hair Hex

This is an old Hungarian beauty spell for gleaming hair and youthful energy.

You will need to gather:

- rosemary essential oil
- sunflower oil
- a sheet of paper
- a red pen
- a sprig of rosemary
- a couple of glasses of spring or mineral water

Dilute 5 drops of rosemary oil in 25 ml of sunflower oil. Massage the mixture into your hair, right down to the ends, while you close your eyes and inhale the scent. Write your name on the paper with the red pen and then dip the sprig of rosemary into a glass of spring water and chant:

> 'Flowery dew and mystic charms,
> bring health and beauty into my arms.'

Soak the paper in the spring water, removing it when the ink has faded. Wash the oil out of your hair with a natural shampoo and use a fresh glass of spring or mineral water as the final rinse.

Good Vibrations

Some essences can be mixed with oils and worn on your body and clothes to attract good fortune and love. One of my favourite oils for mixing is almond, as it also possesses its own enchanted vibration and will help strengthen the energy of your chosen essence. The best time to mix up a magical body oil is on Monday, the day of the Moon, at 7 pm.

Whatever path of the Craft you choose to follow is correct for you because at its highest level, the Craft should always be a path of self-acceptance and freedom of spirit.

Love and Sex Charms

Flower Power

This is a powerful charm to attract a lover towards you.

You will need to gather:

- hibiscuses, (pick three mature flowers and three unopened buds)
- a white cloth
- a cup of red wine
- a pinch of thyme and a pinch of sage
- around 20 cm of copper wire.

Mix a pinch each of thyme and sage in a cup of red wine. Leave the mixture in the Sun for one day. When the Sun goes down, dip your finger into the mixture and use it to paint a stick figure onto the white cloth while you think about your intended lover. Then place all the hibiscus flowers on top of the cloth, roll it up and then tie the bundle up with the piece of copper wire. Next put it outside or near an open window and leave it to be charged by the light of the Moon overnight.

The next day unwrap the bundle, throw away the cloth and wire and bury the flowers near your front door.

Living Goddess

Enliven your bedroom with a 'living' figurehead for love and sexual energy.

You will need to gather:

- *any sized statue (a small one is fine) of your favourite love god or goddess (e.g. Aphrodite, Venus, Pan, Hermes.)*
- *a cup of almond, olive or jojoba oil*
- *a shot of vodka*
- *a teaspoon of mugwort, geranium leaves, comfrey leaves or tea*
- *a pinch of coriander*
- *a sprinkle of salt*

Grind or chop up your herbs and sprinkle them into a bowl along with a shot of vodka and leave them to sit for a few hours. Then pour a cup of almond, olive or jojoba oil on top. With a silver or wooden spoon scoop up three teaspoons of the oil and pour over the god or goddess as you say:

'Welcome to my temple, may you be always in comfort and peace within my home. With the blessing of Holda be now charged with the power of love.'

Then, sprinkle salt around the statue in a clockwise circle and say:

'With this earth you have physical form.'

Next blow breath onto the statue and say:

'With my breath, you shall breathe as I breathe.'

Light a candle and hold it near the statue and say:

'By this sacred fire you are enriched with the spark of life.'

Finally, wash the statue with water and say:

'By the great waters you come to us from across the sea of destiny.'

Finish by wiping the statue dry and sprinkling a few rose or gardenia petals on top and around it. Keep the statue on your altar or in a special area of your bedroom.

The Soulmate Special

To help bring your soulmate into your life.

You will need to gather:

- *a rose quartz crystal*
- *floral perfume*
- *a piece of red cloth*

Take the crystal and hold it close to your chest while you concentrate your thoughts on love and happiness. Feel your heart filling up with emotion as you say:

> *'With crystal clear spirit, through all eternity,*
> *I open my mind and heart to receive true love.*
> *So Shall It Be.'*

Then spray the crystal with the perfume, wrap it in the cloth and keep it near your bed for one to three months.

Pleased To Meet Me

This is a perfect spell to cast if you wish to spark up a romance with either an old acquaintance or a new friend. You will need to first invite your intended lover over to your place and an hour or so before they arrive get dressed in something that contains the colour blue.

You will need to gather:

- an oil burner (the kind that allows you to drop the oils into a water solution and then heat with a candle)
- 3 drops of sandalwood oil
- 3 drops of rose oil (you may substitute rose geranium if you wish)
- 3 drops of orange oil
- 3 drops of jasmine oil

Think about where you would like to entertain your guest and then take the ingredients and oil burner into the chosen room. Next, pour a little water into the oil burner and then, one by one, pour in the drops of the different oils. Light the oil burner candle and then say:

> 'I welcome the warm spirits of my home, and may we be surrounded by feelings of romantic love, may his (her) heart be opened and inspired, O Blessed Be.'

Then go and get ready. Allow the aroma to permeate the room for at least an hour before he or she arrives. (You can also leave the mixture on while they are visiting you, but make sure you turn off the oil burner if you leave the house.)

Circles of Love

To encircle you in waves of love and to attract your chosen one towards you, cast this powerful spell either on a Friday or on the night of a Full Moon.

You will need to gather:

- 🌀 a white plate
- 🌀 a bottle of basil essential oil
- 🌀 a bottle of lemon essential oil
- 🌀 a bottle of musk essential oil
- 🌀 a white candle and a red candle

Find a table or a flat surface to lay all your ingredients on. Put the two candles in holders on either side of the white plate (the white candle on the left, and the red on the right) and light both candles.

Think about the person you want to attract towards you and in your minds eye imagine you see their reflection inside the plate. Next, with the first bottle of essential oil (basil), dab a little bit on your forefinger and wipe a clockwise circle of oil around the entire edge of the plate while you say:

'With the power of one, I cast this circle of love.'

Then do the same thing with the second bottle of oil (lemon verbena), and while wiping a clockwise circle around the plate say:

'With the power of two, I cast this circle of love.'

And finally pick up the last bottle of essential oil (the musk) and wipe a third circle around the plate, while you say:

'With the power of three, the circles are cast, the love will last. So Shall It Be.'

Blow or snuff out the candles and leave the plate in a safe place for seven days. (Straight after the ceremony make sure you wash your hands well to remove all residues of the essential oils, and don't put the oils anywhere near your eyes, as they are very potent.) After seven days, the spell's power will have been sent out into the universe to do its work, so you can then wash the plate in soap and water and use it as normal.

Sexagram

Witchcraft is one of the few spiritual paths that does not separate spirituality from sexuality. In fact, many traditions of the Craft celebrate the merging of the body, mind and spirit and the raising of magical power during the sacred act of sex.

The beautiful and powerful sex rite can be performed to enhance erotic passion between you and your partner, and as an added bonus, the sexual energy raised during lovemaking can be used to empower any type of spell.

You will need to gather:

- some pillows and cushions
- a double bed sheet
- a handful of rose petals
- musk incense
- a few candles
- massage oil of your choice (such as almond or jojoba)

Choose a private room where you can create a magical boudoir for the ritual. Clean an area of the floor and lay down a double bed sheet (it can be in any of your favourite colours). Then lay plenty of cushions and pillows on top and sprinkle a large circle of rose petals (or frangipanis) around everything in a clockwise direction. Dim the lights, put on some sexy background music if you like, and then light the musk incense.

Next, go and have a bath or shower together with your partner, and take your time washing and languishing in the warm water, and when you are both fully relaxed and ready, pat each other dry and remain skyclad and walk back hand in hand into your magical boudoir. If you like, you can light a few candles in the room for extra atmosphere and whenever you are ready, go and stand on either side of the circle of pillows so you are facing each other with your arms and legs apart and looking directly into each other's eyes and begin reciting these incantations.

The woman's first words are:

'Arise O Herne, Hu Gadern.'

The man then answers:

'I am Herne, your horned god, your stag has risen
from the sacred woodlands.'

The woman answers:

'Herne, you are my stag, you are my ram, my sacred temple
is moist and open, come and let's ignite the astral flame.'

Then both come into the circle and get comfortable on the pillows and start kissing and caressing and anointing each other's bodies with the massage oil (almond or jojoba or one of your own choosing).

The rest of this powerfully potent ritual is up to your own sexy imagination, but if you do want to use the raised energy for magic during your lovemaking, then when either or both of you are at the point of orgasm, focus your mind on the purpose of your spell to help send it zooming off into the Universe.

Fertility Magic

Since time began, women have been making lucky charms and casting fertility spells to help them conceive their dream baby.

Many of these old traditions follow the cycles of the Sun and the Moon, as well as the connection between Mother Nature and Goddess Magic. The ancient spellcasters observed that the Moon has a definite link to female fertility and created many charms that could harness the power of the goddess Luna.

Remember that your female cycle follows the 12 lunar months. Find out when your monthly ovulation time is and perform this spell then.

You will need to gather:

◎ apple-scented body cream
◎ a silver necklace

Take a relaxing shower (ideally a romantic one with your partner) and then, with your partner, gently massage the apple-scented body cream into your skin, paying extra attention to your tummy area. Imagine as you rub in the cream that your and your partner's hands are glowing with a mystic silver light which is filling this area with life and power. Actually visualise yourself pregnant as your partner gently places the necklace around your neck and you repeat these Magic words together:

'Silvery goddess, o shining Luna,
I wear your precious light.
Let fertile power glow through me.
O Blessed Be This Night.'

Fertile Phases

Many Celtic magicians believe that a woman is most fertile for the three days around the same phase of the Moon as she was born under. In other words, if you were born during a New Moon, then you should be most fertile during a New Moon; if you were born during a Full Moon, you are most fertile during that time.

Love Potion

Excellent for spells of romance and fertility.

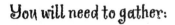

You will need to gather:

- romantic music
- 2 gold-coloured goblets
- red wine or fruit drink
- gardenia and rose petals
- geranium essential oil
- an oil burner

Have some sexy fun by casting this spell with your partner. At midnight on a Friday, take a shower together and both dress in light clothing. Play some romantic music and fill the goblets with the wine or fruit drink. Prepare the bedroom beforehand by scattering the flower petals over the freshly made bed. Burn the geranium essence and, after you each take a sip from the goblets, repeat this incantation:

> 'Bacchus, god of wine and fun, Make our wishes come true
> And fill our days with wonder.'

If you wish to conceive a child, an ancient Sun ritual for babymaking is to place some yellow feathers and an orange scarf under the bed before you make love.

A Boy or a Girl?

For centuries it has been recognised that astrological signs tend to have either a masculine or feminine nature. To help you choose the sex of your baby, buy a calendar which shows the 12 astrological phases and cast your fertility spell during the best star time to conceive either a boy or a girl.

For a boy, choose Masculine Signs

Aries
Gemini
Leo
Libra
Sagittarius
Aquarius

For a girl, choose Feminine Signs

Taurus
Cancer
Virgo
Scorpio
Capricorn
Pisces

A Little Ray of Sunshine

In all cultures, the Sun has been revered and honoured as the bringer of life and fertile energy. Connect with the eternal power of Apollo the Sun god by casting this spell at noon at the beginning of the most fertile time of the month for you.

You will need to gather:

- *a white tablecloth*
- *a vase of yellow rosebuds*
- *a few seashells*
- *a bay leaf*

Prepare a love altar in your bedroom by placing the tablecloth and rosebuds on a table or your dresser along with the seashells.

Hold the bay leaf—which is also ruled by the Sun—in your hand for a few moments while you sit calmly near your altar. Gaze at the rosebuds and visualise them starting to open and bloom. As you do this, imagine that your whole body is blooming and opening up like a beautiful flower, and repeat this incantation:

'Golden Apollo, from this enchanted hour,
let me open to fertile seed,
help me receive love's Magic power.'

To seal the spell's power, place the bay leaf under your pillow before you make love with your partner.

Enchanted Sun Kisses

Each week on the day of the Sun (Sunday), sit outside in the light or near an open window and roll an orange around your tummy as you say:

'Sun kissed with Nature's bliss
help me to conceive.'

Then kiss the orange three times, cut it into quarters and eat it with breakfast or lunch.

Special Seeds

Another old Magic charm is for couples to sprinkle uncooked rice or sunflower seeds under the marital bed to aid fertility.

Basil For Babies

Add a Magic dash of basil to your dinner to spice up your chances of conception.

Once you learn to

tap into your

inner power,

it can really

change your life.

Dream Weaver

The ancient alchemists understood that 'when the body sleeps the soul awakens' and that our dreams are a magical source of inspiration, guidance and prophecy. Dreams are just like secret messages from our spiritual self. They give us information on what is really happening deep in our subconscious mind and the universe around us. With these dream spells and enchanted rituals you can also learn to tap into the power of your dreams—to show you how to best deal with everyday problems and to give you important insights into the past and the future.

Remembering Your Dreams

We can all learn how to remember our dreams more clearly by following these mindpower and focusing techniques.

Firstly, make sure that you go to sleep in a quiet environment, without the interference or distraction of outside noises. If you do fall asleep while watching TV or listening to the radio, your dreaming pattern will take on some of what you have seen and heard, and will not be a real insight into your subconscious.

Start a Dream Workbook. Put a new diary and pen near your bed and as soon as you wake up in the morning, write down immediately any images or emotions you had while you slept.

Before you go to sleep, sit on your bed and breathe calmly and deeply for a moment or two to relax and then repeat this incantation:

> *'Peace and understanding flow this night,*
> *O Universe, let me remember my dreams*
> *and clear my second sight.'*

Dream Numbers

Half an hour or so before you go to bed, sit on a chair in front of a mirror and look at your own reflection as you repeat this incantation:

> *'I am grateful for life,*
> *and I know that wealth and prosperity*
> *are within me.'*

Then, on a notepad, write down all of the numbers from one to 100 as you breathe calmly and let go of worries and stress. Turn over the page so you have a clean, new piece of paper and as you get into bed, place the notebook and a pen nearby so you can easily write down any numbers that come to you in your dreams.

Sleepy Solutions

You know that old saying 'Go and sleep on it'? Well, it is true that while we sleep we can call on our higher wisdom to help make big decisions and solve all sorts of problems.

To do this, before you go to bed write your problem or question on a red piece of paper. Sit in a quiet place, hold the paper in front of you, and gaze at the colour of the paper and the words you have written.

Don't think about your problem or anything else; relax your mind and let yourself absorb the warmth and vibrancy of the colour.

Then, just before you lie down, tear the paper into pieces and sprinkle them and some chamomile tea leaves under your bed. In the morning you will start to feel an answer to your important question forming.

An old Celtic charm for insightful dreams is to sprinkle salt under the four corners of the bed and walk clockwise around your bedroom three times with your question in mind.

Wealthy Dreaming

To bring forth dreams of wealth and insights into career direction, cast this spell on the night of a New or Full Moon.

Place some white carnation petals and geranium leaves under your pillow and say:

'Shasheeta, goddess of the mystic light,
lead me to my rightful path.
Show me the way
to my rightful abundance and prosperity.'

Repeat this spell once a week for the next month.

Enchanted Dream Herbs

There are a few wonderful old herbs that can help you achieve many things while dreaming—like flying, astral travelling and visualising your soulmate.

Before you go to bed, put a teaspoon or a teabag of the chosen herb into a cup of hot water and let it steep for 5 minutes. As you sip your tea, imagine that your body is feeling lighter and more tranquil.

- *Rosehip: superb for love and soulmate dreaming*
- *Valerian: wonderful for deep, healing dreams*
- *Mulberry: for dreams of flying and astral travel*

No Nightmares Elixir

A Magic potion to guard against nightmares can be made by mixing a teaspoon of apple-cider vinegar and a teaspoon of honey into a small cup of warm water and sipping this elixir slowly before bedtime.

Facing Your Demons

Whenever you have dreams about being chased, try to find the courage to stop running, and turn to face your pursuer. You will find that it's actually yourself and your inner fears trying to be understood and resolved.

Viewing The Future

To evoke dreams of future gazing and prediction, wear an amethyst crystal or moonstone on a chain or leather strap around your neck at night.

Dream Symbols

The memorable images and pictures in your dreams often hold hidden meaning and cosmic messages.

You will often have one main teaching dream each night, and these are a few of the symbols that may appear:

MALE AND FEMALE FIGURES:
represent your masculine and feminine sides

ROOMS IN A HOUSE OR FLAT:
represent the different chambers of your subconscious and memories

CHILDREN AND BABIES:
represent your inner child needing to be listened to

ANIMALS:
represent the different feelings you have about a situation
(for instance, a wolf or shark would represent danger,
a snake or horse usually suggests passion and sexuality)

A PET OR A RELATIVE WHO HAS PASSED AWAY:
you are about to receive important news

In Magic nothing is impossible! It is really just a matter of spending time learning and applying the natural laws of the universe on a daily basis.

Wikid Ways

There is nothing like a cup of brew, a hex and a good lie down. I'd recommend it to anyone who's had a hard day at the office, has been stuck in bumper-to-bumper traffic or has just gone through a difficult divorce.

High-heeled Hexer

There are times when you may experience some unwanted 'shadow passing', which is when other people either consciously or unconsciously pass their own dark shadows and fears over to us, and you may be especially vulnerable to this during or after a relationship break-up. Cast this spell if you feel as if an ex-friend or lover has been sending you their dark shadows or especially when you have been left emotionally bruised and traumatised by a messy break-up or divorce.

You will need to gather:

- for women: you will need a pair of red or black high-heeled shoes (stilettos are perfect)
- for men: you can wear a pair of boots (cuban heel or cowboy boots are great, but any boots will do)
- a photograph of the 'shadow passer' or a piece of paper and a pen.

At the stroke of midnight during a Waning Moon or Diminishing Moon, take the photograph or write the name of the shadow passer onto the piece of paper three times and go to a private place where you will be undisturbed. Get completely undressed. Remain skyclad and put on your high-heeled shoes. Keep the lights on and go and stand in front of a mirror. Look at your reflection in the

mirror and breathe very calmly and deeply, and concentrate only on positive and uplifting thoughts.

Next, take the photograph or the piece of paper, and put it down on the floor. Stand over it with your legs apart so you are directly over the picture and looking down at it, and then say these words with conviction:

'A woman (man) scorned is a sight to behold,
A woman's (man's) fury can turn fire cold,
When I gave you my sweet love
    you gave me your deepest shadow,
But now at my feet your shadow I see
And I name and return it straight back
    from whence it came.'

Then stamp on the photo or paper three times with your left heel and then three times with your right heel. When you've done that, stand up with your arms raised and, looking to the heavens, say:

'Your shadow is finally released from me
and may it now return and serve you
in the name of love and good will,
O Blessed Be.'

To finish, throw the photo or paper into the garbage bin, and then go and either soak in a warm bath or have a refreshing shower to cleanse any leftover tensions and negative energy. Then go to bed for a well-deserved and restful night's sleep.

Home Protection

You will need to gather:

- ✒ a mirror
- ✒ a handful of sage
- ✒ fresh white sheets and coverlet
- ✒ some white flowers (such as daisies or gardenias) in two vases

To help the energy of your home flow properly, place the mirror on the back inside wall of your living room and, while holding the sage in your hand, walk clockwise around the main rooms of the house three times with your mind focused on positive thoughts as you repeat this incantation:

> 'Love before me, love beside me, love behind me,
> bring peace, harmony and truth.'

Make your bed with the fresh sheets and coverlet and place the flowers in your living room and bedroom.

It is also helpful to paint the front doors or windowsills light blue and to place some red carnations in a flower pot near the front entrance.

Give Up the Ghost

If you think there may be some strange energies in your home or you feel there may even be a leftover spirit or ghost, cast this 'happy ghost' spell.

On the stroke of midnight, light a white candle, hold a cup of spring water and sit in front of a mirror as you gaze in silence into the reflected light. Breathe in deeply a few times and then call the Angel of the Air, Earth, Water and Fire by sprinkling a few drops of the water around you and repeating this incantation:

*'Heavenly angels hear my request,
release those spirits from their earthly bounds.'*

Concentrate on happy thoughts and, as you blow out the candle, say:

'And now you are at rest, it will be so, O Blessed Be.'

Happy Halloween

Halloween, or Allhallows Eve, was one of the most important festivals in old Europe for magicians and spellcasters because midnight on October 31 was traditionally when everyone counted their blessings for the year and the spirit world and the 'real' world got together for a big party. In ancient Europe it was called Samhain, and marked the end of one Druid year and the beginning of the next. Nowadays, Halloween is celebrated everywhere, and many children and adults have lots of fun dressing up as witches and goblins or their favourite characters from Hollywood movies. In Australia and elsewhere in the Southern Hemisphere many witches celebrate Halloween and Samhain on April 30. Whatever day you choose to follow to help you get into the celebratory spirit of Halloween, here are some spells and Magic tips to make your party memorable.

During the day of Halloween pick 13 leaves from a tree—one for each of the 13 Full Moons—and place them in a wooden or cardboard box as you recite this Halloween chant:

> 'O gracious goddess, I thank you for all your bounty,
> as the wheel turns, walk with me from season to season
> through night and day.'

Then place the box somewhere in your bedroom, maybe under your bed. This will ensure that you have lots of love and prosperity during the coming year.

In ancient times, Halloween was ruled by the goddess Pomona whose symbol is the fruit tree. To invoke the healing and loving energy of Pomona, cast this Magic apple spell at noon or midnight.

Cut up an apple into nine equal parts. Eat eight of the segments and then throw the ninth over your left shoulder as you say:

> 'Spirits and Magic fairies and elves,
> send good fortune to all our friends.'

If you're thinking of having a Halloween party, here are some tricks and treats for your guests to have fun with.

Keep the lights low and hang lots of party lanterns and fairy lights.

Set up a gypsy table in a corner of the room, complete with a crystal ball or a tarot card reader, and watch how many of your guests line up for a reading.

Many party shops sell spray-on fake cobwebs and plastic flying bats, both of which create a fabulous atmosphere in hallways. Hang some over the front door as well.

Bang tambourines and ring bells as a traditional way to celebrate Halloween. These instruments are often used by mediums to help bring friendly spirits into a room.

Make your own witch's broomstick by tying up one or more straw brooms with red, white and green ribbons. Then sweep your front doorstep with each of the brooms to help get rid of old problems and worries. Leave the brooms near the front and back doors during the party for good luck.

No Halloween party is complete without some Jack O'Lantern pumpkins placed in a window or lined up along the garden path. If you want to go all out, scoop out the inside of the pumpkin and carve in a smiling face. A much easier way is to paint a smiling face on the outside, then scoop out the middle. For extra effect you can burn a tealight candle inside while you recite:

> 'With this candle and by its light
> I welcome ye Spirits this Halloween night.'

To get you and your guests into a party mood, serve some homemade enchanted Halloween Lemon Wine.

Pour a bottle of white wine into a punch bowl. Add one large bottle of lemonade and stir with a wooden spoon as you say:

> 'Bring joy and lightness on Allhallows Eve,
> begin the Magic on Halloween.'

Then slice up three or four lemons and add to the wine mixture along with a packet of maraschino cherries.
Serve chilled with ice in long glasses.

Broken Mirror

If you break a mirror, sprinkle salt and rosemary over the pieces, sweep them up carefully and throw them into the garbage bin. Then light a stick of sandalwood incense and walk anticlockwise around the bin seven times as you say:

> 'One year gone of bad luck,
> now two, three, four, five, six and seven.'

Then walk clockwise around the bin as you say:

> 'Powers of the Universe,
> bring good fortune for one year, and two,
> three, four, five, six and seven.
> So Be It.'

Wands of Merlin

This fun party game uses 'wands' similar to divining sticks. The Wands of Merlin are made from small pieces of wood and are excellent tools for looking into the future and obtaining a quick 'yes' or 'no' answer to an important question.

Collect seven wooden sticks of exactly the same length (skewers or chopsticks will do fine).

Make a space on the floor of one of the party rooms for a large piece of white cardboard which has a straight line drawn straight across the middle. Stand at least 30 cm away from the straight line and hold all seven of the sticks in your right hand. Close your eyes as you think about your important question. When you are ready, open your eyes and quickly throw the sticks towards the line drawn on the cardboard. Next, count how many sticks are above the line and how many are below. If there are more above the line, your answer is 'yes', if there are more below, your answer is 'no'.

Soul Serenity

A magical time for rest and reflection, and for this self-esteem booster.

On the day of a Full or New Moon, revive your aura by dabbing on some orange essential oil in a little carrier oil and dressing in some mauve or purple clothing. Sit in front of an open window and breathe in and out deeply for a few moments to calm your body and mind. Rest your hands on your knees with your palms facing upwards and repeat this incantation:

'Deep within me, my soul is my guide.
I shall put away my fears and know
that I deserve to fulfil my dreams
and follow my true purpose.
I open my mind and heart
in the flow of universal love.
O Blessed Be.'

Leave Me Be

Cast this spell to banish any negative energies or to protect you from bothersome people.

You will need to gather:

- ✎ I cup of white flour
- ✎ I cup of goat's milk or yoghurt
- ✎ a piece of paper
- ✎ a pen
- ✎ some old potato skins
- ✎ a piece of fish
- ✎ a garbage bag

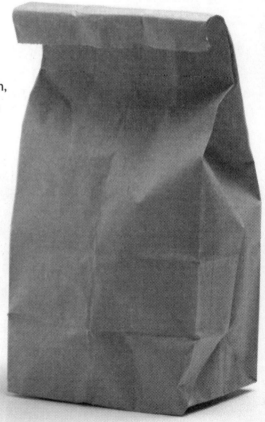

On the night of a Full or Diminishing Moon, make some dough using the flour and goat's milk or yoghurt, kneading it until you have a firm mixture. Take the piece of paper and write the name of the bothersome person three times, then press it into the middle of the dough. Roll the dough into a ball and place it and the potato skins and a piece of fish inside a garbage bag as you say:

'The powers that be
send me a sacred spell,
to leave me alone will do you well'.

Throw the garbage bag into the garbage bin while you concentrate on letting go of negative thoughts and worries.

Kid Power

Children live in quite a different world from most adults. They absorb life like a sponge, their active minds still fresh and full of wonder at the universe around them. This is the time in their lives when they really should be encouraged to believe in their dreams and their own creative abilities. But nowadays, with the rise of technology, computer games and too much television, children can start to lose valuable playtime in which to practise their natural fantasies and intuition. With these simple Magic rituals and games, you will not only bring out the imagination and self-expression of your child, but may also rediscover your own wonderful enchanted world.

Magical Beginnings

This is a beautiful way to bring Magic to a child's christening or baby-naming ceremony. You will use items that represent the four magical elements: Earth, Water, Fire and Air.

You will need to gather:

- a white candle
- a bowl of spring water
- a bowl of earth
- a white feather

Begin the ceremony by placing the four items on a table. Light the candle and hold the feather in your right hand as you look over towards the family gathering and say:

'Hail and welcome.
We have come together to celebrate the naming of this precious child.
By Water and Earth you shall love the animals
    and learn the wisdom of Nature.
By Fire and Air, you will walk safely through all places.
May the Universal Spirit, God and Goddess bless and protect you
    as you grow in the light of love.'

Sweet Dreams

To help your child sleep peacefully and have pleasant dreams, create a tranquil and calming environment in their bedroom.

The windows should have light-coloured, pastel-toned curtains and walls, and the bedhead should be well away from the door. Cleanse the atmosphere by holding some vanilla incense and walking through the room with a peaceful mind and heart. At bedtime, turn off anything distracting or disturbing, such as the TV, loud music or radios. Put a lavender sachet under your child's pillow and, as you tuck them into bed, say:

'Feather light on starry night,
cosy warm and tired,
pleasant dreams and sweetest thoughts
as little angels smile.'

Enchanted Birthday

Children's birthday parties are a perfect time for wishing spells and lucky charms. After all, we all still practise the ancient tradition of making a wish as we blow out our birthday candles.

To add a special touch of Magic to the celebration, fill the room with lots of balloons in your child's favourite colour tied with green and white ribbons for luck. To help attract good fortune and fairy Magic, sprinkle glitter and rose petals or scented potpourri around the table.

Hang a mirror somewhere on the wall so the elves can see the food and drinks, and don't forget lots of fairy cakes and bread sprinkled with hundreds and thousands.

For extra enchantment, remember that pixies are supposed to be very fond of lemonade, strawberries and small bells.

You can also buy a Magic wishing book for your child and place it near the front door. Each of the party guests should sign their name in the book, near the words:

> 'As your birthday guest and
>   friend so true,
> I say your wishes will come true.'

Magic Wand

What could be more fabulous for a child than to have their own Magic wand? Instead of buying one, help them make their own special wand, which will be more effective.

Go outside together to a garden or park (preferably on a Sunday or on the morning of a Growing Moon) and search for a slim stick that appeals to your child. Hazel or hawthorn is the ancient traditional wood, but if you can't find these trees you can use the Druid's favourite, a twig from an oak tree. If you live in the Southern Hemisphere, you can use a stick from one of the native species for a highly effective Magic tool.

Take the stick home and let the child really use their imagination to decorate it with beads and feathers (or anything they desire) tied on firmly with white, purple or gold string. You could also show them how to glue on some stars and moons and lots of glitter. When they have finished, leave the wand near a window for one day and one night to absorb the light of the Sun and Moon. Then let the child charge it with their own personal Magic by holding it in the air as they turn clockwise in a circle and say:

*'I charge this wand for the good of all
in the name of love and Magic.'*

Tossing Cares Away

If your child is being bothered at school or is not getting along with some other kids, show them this lovely charm.

Take some cottonwool balls, sprinkle them with a tiny dash of talcum powder, and have your child sit in a quiet, light-filled space while they breathe calmly and let their mind and body relax. Ask them to close their eyes and then put a few of the cottonwool balls in their hands and let them feel the softness of the fluffy cotton and gently breathe their cares away. Next, ask them to repeat after you these words:

> 'Softer, lighter, one, two, three,
> problems float away from me.
> I have friends who care about me
> and I am as lucky as can be.'

Then, open a door or a window and help your child to throw the cottonwool balls outside, just as if they were throwing away all their worries and cares.

Self-esteem Builder

I receive many letters from parents and their children who are concerned about passing their school exams. This self-esteem charm will help release stress and give them the ability to focus on their studies.

You will need to gather:

- a mirror
- a clear quartz crystal
- a crayon or old lipstick

On any morning or evening, have your child sit in front of a mirror so they can see their own reflection. Put the crystal on a table or flat surface nearby. Ask them to think about what they would like to achieve in the future or in their exams, and let them write that on the mirror surface. Next, ask them to concentrate on looking at themselves in the mirror and letting go of all worries so they feel calm and positive, and then repeat these words:

'I am unique and special,
I am loved by the Universe
and I have a clever mind.
When I believe in myself,
I can create wonderful things around me,
I can do anything and I believe in me.'

They can then keep the crystal in their room or school bag and so they can repeat this spell whenever they feel like it.

Your spirit is eternal and is connected with all knowledge and wisdom in the universe.

Animal Magic

Most people adore their pets, especially their cats and dogs. And Nature - lovers and Good Witches (including me) are no exception. As well as being great company, cats and dogs are quite psychic and can sense with uncanny accuracy when their owners need some extra love and affection, and without any prompting will often know when family members are about to arrive home or need some extra protection. We consider our pets to be part of our family, so why not cast a few Magic spells to help keep them healthy and happy?

One of the most enchanted days of the week to cast pet spells is on Saturday, the day of Saturn, because it rules over Nature and its cycles. Another especially Magic time is when the moon is in the Earth signs of Capricorn, Virgo and Taurus.

Animal Protection

To keep good energy and healthy vibrations around your cat or dog, buy a cat's-eye crystal and a moonstone from a crystal shop and wash them in spring water on the day of a New or Growing Moon. Dry the stones thoroughly with a clean, white cloth. Hold the stones in your right hand and walk clockwise three times around your pet, softly repeating this incantation:

'Magico Mystico, bring forth your circle of power,
protect my beloved (say the name of your pet)
from this day on and every hour. O Blessed Be.'

Then keep the stones in a glass or earthenware jar near your front door.

Doggy Patrol

Is your pooch a wanderer? If so, you can draw in some protective energy by making a special charm for him to wear.

The colour brown is good for animals, as it soothes their auras, so buy your dog a brown collar, preferably made of leather, and as you place it around his neck, say:

'San Francesco, protect this animal from harm.'

Then, before you attach his identification tag to the collar, hold the tag in your hand and focus your mind on seeing a warm, happy glow around him as you repeat this incantation:

'While you wear this charm
may you never stray far from home.'

Communicating With Your Cat

Cats have been known for centuries as psychic and mystical creatures, and your family moggy is no exception. If you'd like to know what your cat is thinking or perhaps bring him/her into your Magic circle, try this spell at midnight on the night of a Full Moon.

You will need to gather:

- ✐ a handful of aniseeds
- ✐ a mortar and pestle or a wooden bowl and spoon
- ✐ 1 teaspoon of valerian tea leaves
- ✐ a small cotton or cheesecloth square
- ✐ some blue ribbon

Place your spell items on a table, grind the aniseeds with the mortar and pestle or the bowl and spoon, and then mix in the valerian tea as you recite the words:

> 'By the eye of the cat,
> by the wing of the bat,
> be clean and clear.
> Bring the familiar spirit near.'

Finish your spell by pouring the mixture onto the cheesecloth and tying up the ends with the ribbon. Wear this bag in your pocket when you're playing with your cat or simply hang it near its bed.

Fly Away Fleas

An old charm to keep your dog or cat free from fleas is to pour two cups of mineral water into a bowl and mix in one drop each of sage, cedar and fennel essential oils. Stir the potion counterclockwise with a wooden spoon as you say these Magic words aloud:

'Fly away fleas, begone I say,
don't come back another day!'

Then sprinkle some of the mixture directly over your pet's coat or onto a brush and comb carefully over its entire fur.

Healing Spell

When your trusted dog or cat has to visit the vet, you can cast this charm to help speed up the healing or to calm its nerves.

Light some sandalwood incense and a brown and green candle. Sit quietly nearby with your pet and speak quietly to it and gently stroke its fur for a few moments. As you do this, say the name of the animal goddess Bast (for a cat) or Brigit (if it's a dog) nine times, and then say:

'I call on the guardian Goddess
to care and protect this animal.
Bring health and comfort
and allow them to be well in the eyes
of Nature.'

Pet Charms

Catnip: helps create a bond between you and your cat; place it in a wooden box or in a drawstring pouch when you are playing together.

Vervain: scatter over your garden or footpath to quieten a barking dog.

Meditating Moggy

For a more spiritual and tranquil cat, sprinkle some catnip and oregano into a brown drawstring bag and make a smaller sachet for your cat. Wear yours for three days around your neck while you are meditating with your puddy for at least 15 minutes a day. You can either tie the pet's sachet to its collar while you meditate, or place it near the cat. After those three days, take all the herbs and throw them into the wind at midday or midnight.

If you wish to try this with your dog, use rosemary instead of catnip and add a dash of chamomile.

Power Paws

An old folk charm to help stop a straying pet is to rub a little pure butter onto its front paws once a month during a Full or New Moon.

If you are going on holiday and you have to leave your pet with friends or at a boarding kennel, be sure to pack a photo of you and your pet together, along with one or two of their hairs in a matchbox. This is said to stop them fretting for you too much.

The beauty of Magic is that you can weave your spells and charms wherever and wherever you want to.

Broomstick Travel

Are you just itching to get away on a romantic weekend for two? Or perhaps a trip on your own around the world is your idea of seventh heaven. Whether you dream of lazing on a tropical island or kicking up your heels in a big city, you can help make your dreams come true by weaving a little travel Magic.

Neptune's Wish

If your wish is to go on a fabulous holiday near the sea, cast this spell at midday on a Sunday.

Stand near a pond or a stretch of water, holding a ginger root and some seaweed in your hand. Try to focus your mind on where you would like to go and as you gaze into the water, repeat this incantation:

> 'By the power of Neptune,
> by the Gods of the sea.
> Grant me a good journey
> and so shall it be.'

Throw the ginger and the seaweed into the water, then close your eyes and imagine that you are already on your holiday by the sea, smelling the salty air, strolling along the beach and having a great time.

Bon Voyage Balm

To help make sure you are feeling healthy and fit for your holiday, perform this Magic ritual on either a day of a New Moon or a Sunday.

You will need to gather:

- 2 blue candles
- an oil burner
- lavender essential oil
- rosemary essential oil
- bergamot essential oil (optional)
- a sheet of paper
- a blue pen

Light the candles and oil burner, adding a few drops of the lavender and rosemary oils (and a few drops of bergamot to bring in more vibrations of healing). Stand to the right side of the room, raise your arms above your head and look up to the ceiling as you call in the positive energy forces by repeating this incantation:

'Great healing powers,
come directly to me,
fill me with strength and vigour.
In return I will send out
gratitude to the Universe.'

Next, take the piece of paper and use the blue pen to write down your travel destination and when you plan to go. Read this through a few times and then say with confidence:

'As I prepare for my trip
I will be well and fit.'

Leave the candles and oils burning for another minute or two, then as you blow them out, say:

'It Will Be So.'

200

Travelling Star

If you or a loved one is going away, cast this protection charm for a safe and happy journey.

Seven days before the trip, put seven hazelnuts into a green cloth and tie up the ends with a piece of string while you focus on positive and happy thoughts and repeat this incantation:

> 'One, my wish is for smooth travelling,
> two, my wish is for comfort,
> three, my wish is for a safe journey,
> four, my wish is for good weather,
> five, my wish is for fun,
> six, my wish is for wonderful memories,
> and seven, Oh Travelling Star, guide us all safely home.'

Then place the pouch into one of the luggage bags and sprinkle a pinch of salt over all the rest of the luggage for luck.

Jetsetter

If you suffer from fear of flying, then take these charms with you on your flight. Hold on to them whenever you need some strength and tranquillity.

A week or so before you go on your trip, collect a piece of amber, a clear quartz, and a tiger's-eye or cat's-eye crystal (available at crystal shops) and leave them soaking in a glass of milk for one night.

In the morning, wash them with mineral water and, after drying them thoroughly, hold them in your hands and repeat this incantation:

> 'Hermes, Pegasus, Gods of Luck and Flight,
> protect me from this moment
> and guide the plane through darkness
> and light.'

Take the crystals with you in a blue pouch and you'll be up there with the rest of the jetsetters in no time.

Magic Planet

Confused about where you should go on your trip? Cast this spell at 10 am on any day.

Gather around you some magazine clippings and travel brochures of exotic and exciting locations from around the world. Then find a Y-shaped branch from a tree. After you have placed the pictures around you in a semicircle, grasp the short ends of the branch with your hands and allow the long end to tip downwards near the brochures as you say:

> 'Apollo and Zeus guide my hand
> as this branch lands,
> joy and pleasure shall be mine
> and adventure I will find.'

Close your eyes for a moment and let the branch move from side to side. When you feel a strong pull in any direction, stop the branch there and open your eyes to see your travel destination revealed.

Magic Travel Tips

For some enchanting gift ideas for travelling friends, try to find copies of old maps of the world or an old-style compass. Velvet or cotton shoe bags in lucky colours such as green and blue also make magical presents.

To empower your gifts, buy them on Wednesday, the day of the God of journeys and communication, Mercury.

To help boost your own holiday finances, gather green clover on the night or day of a New Moon and sprinkle in a circle around your bank statements.

To attract money and savings, each day before your trip wrap a one-dollar coin in silver foil and put it inside an old money purse that has been dusted with a pinch of cinnamon.

Business Booster

Not all journeys are for holidays. If you're going on an important business trip, give yourself a bit of extra luck on the way.

Before you leave on your trip, bless your credit cards and business documents with this lucky spell.

Cast your Magic on a Sunday, preferably in the sunlight. The Sun encourages more 'gold' and can help attract success into your life. Gather together your documents and cards and wrap them in a bright yellow or gold-coloured scarf. Place the bundle on a flat surface, light a stick of frankincense and wave it over the bundle as you visualise your future business meeting. Keep your thoughts positive and upbeat as you repeat this incantation:

'Solar Magic here begins,
from Apollo's chariot flies
success to win.'

Fly Away

There are some ancient recipes for 'flying ointment' which were used for broomsticks, but since we are modern Magic Spinners, we much prefer travelling by jet. I use this one whenever I want to get a good seat on a plane, but you can also use it for attracting a job in aviation.

You will need to gather:

- a small bowl
- 1 teaspoon of jojoba oil
- 1 teaspoon of sunflower oil
- 2 drops of jasmine essential oil
- a silver spoon
- 1 chicken stock cube
- a clean jar with a lid

On the night of a Full Moon, mix together in the bowl the jojoba and sunflower oils and jasmine essential oil with the silver spoon as you concentrate on seeing yourself happily sitting in your favourite seat on the plane or working in your flight attendant's uniform, and repeat this incantation:

> 'Silver of Mercury my night-time Sun,
> in Moonlight's power enchantment has begun.'

Then crumble half the stock cube and sprinkle a little bit into the oil as you say:

> 'Birds of a feather, I call thee nigh!
> With Magic's touch I will soon fly.'

Wipe a tiny bit of the ointment behind your knees and keep the rest of it in the jar.

Universal Compass

This ritual will help you align with the Universal energies and the four cardinal directions wherever you are in the galaxies.

Instead of trying to work out the four directions with a mechanical compass, in your mind's eye imagine instead that your actual body is a compass—with your head North, your right hand East, your feet South and your left hand West.

Stand up straight, with your feet in a comfortable position and with both arms stretched out to either side. Keep the 'body compass' image in mind as you then 'see' the colour of pure spiritual white glowing in your 'North' head position. Then 'see' and feel that the colour red is glowing warm and vibrant like the Sun in your left hand, which is East, and the colour blue is feeling like cool and refreshing water in your left hand in the West, while in the South at your feet, the colour brown is helping to 'ground' and connect you with earth. Feel yourself align with the four directions and feel the different temperatures and natures of each of the four colours.

Play around as long as you like with these elements and see how they each give you a different sensation and feeling.

Allow yourself to soar up to the sky with the feeling of white 'airiness' in your mind and then bring this feeling down through to the centre of your body, around your stomach area, and bring in some colour red and some of the blue to do a bit of self-healing and energising.

When you feel ready to finish your ritual, think about the colour brown at your feet in the South, and see how it helps to ground you.

Let yourself finish with a sense that your are now in a place of balance and strength.

my life as a witch

a magical journey

The beginning ~ A witch in the Castle of Oz ~ A model witchling ~ The inner witch blossoms ~ Meeting the Druid Master ~ Hex in the city

part *four*

The beginning

My Magical journey began when I was a young child, growing up with my freedom- and Nature-loving family. In fact, my early attraction to all things Magical was hardly surprising considering my ancestry and family background. Ours is a mixed heritage—a hybrid of Celtic and Anglo-Saxon roots, interestingly enough, the same path I have subconsciously chosen for practice of the Craft.

On my father's side there are Scots and Irish gypsies, who were very much the Bards of the family—travelling minstrels, poets and actors. Some of my father's clan travelled from Ireland in the late 1600s to countries all over the world, and it is thought that quite a few of them ended up as far away as Canada and New England. In fact, just recently I met a namesake of our 'Tutty' clan who lives in Canada, and who is a talented musician and a Magical performer of Celtic and Druidic songs. Dad's own great-great-grandparents migrated to Australia from Ireland and the British Isles in the mid-1800s, and many of that family had also been well known throughout Europe as musicians, dancers and theatre performers. Some even went on to become part of the early vaudeville history of Australia and worked with the legendary 'Mo' as well as Americans such as Harry Houdini and W.C. Fields.

Way back in the early 1900s, Australia was considered to be the last frontier for the gypsy life of vaudeville, and many international entertainers eagerly came here on ships, to tour alongside the local performers. They didn't only perform in major cities, either. Many braved long journeys on horses with the bullock trains to perform in small country towns, putting up their tents and hauling their caravans along the roughest of dirt tracks throughout the Aussie outback.

Among them were also a number of psychics and mediums (in the old days they use to be called spiritualists and fortune-tellers), and as a child I sat listening to my grandparents and parents passing on the stories of all these Magical adventures from the old days, as well as the Bardic-style verses and songs that have helped keep our family's traditions and our Celtic heritage well and truly alive.

My mother's ancestry is Anglo-Welsh and Cornish, and it is common knowledge in her family that we had an 'aunty witch' back in Wales sometime in the 1800s. From what my uncle tells me, she was the village herbalist and wore a pointy black hat (probably just the Welsh folk costume) and practised her own form of veterinary medicine, as well as mixing up various potions and salves for the village folk. (And I wonder why I get such a kick out of stirring up my own love potions…) Actually, I don't think she had such a penchant for love potions. Apparently, old Aunty never married and lived happily by herself in a tiny wooden house with a dirt floor—which she swept out regularly with a big straw broom, of course.

I could go on forever about all the unique characters on both sides of my family, but it's probably sufficient to say that I've had quite a few important Magical guides and mentors in my life, including my parents and ancestors. And that was a great start to my life of being a Real Witch. Before I learnt much else, I was taught to have great respect and wonder for all things spiritual and mystical.

A Witch In The Castle Of Oz

I always knew about my witchy side but the first time I really understood the power of my own will was when I landed a job as an assistant to our nation's big Wiz, the Australian Prime Minister.

One moment I was a 15-year-old schoolgirl dreamily gazing out of the window of my typing class, occasionally listening to the government employment scout as he whizzed by in his brown safari suit and handed us kids our sign-up forms—each one with a neat list of secretarial jobs numbered one to 100. 'Just pick your first, second and third choices for an exciting career in the Commonwealth Government,' he said.

And can you guess which one I cheekily placed a big tick next to? Why numero uno, of course! My first choice was for the top job available: Secretary to the Prime Minister.

You see, at that time I was having serious second thoughts about having given in to the 'Mum knows best' rave and gone to do this secretarial and typing course in the first place ('In case you need something to fall back on, dear'). I'd be leaving school just to end up sitting in some obscure typing pool? I don't think so. Nope, if I couldn't land the top job, I'd be giving up on this line of work entirely. So I firmly ticked my first and only choice: number one. My rationale was, if I wasn't going to be invited into the VIP room, why bother even going to their party?

Abracadabra and one, two, three

clicks of Dorothy's red shoes, and the next thing I know I'm striding through the hallways of Parliament House. But this little Dorothy is now wearing her brand-new white lace-up boots and faux-suede mini-skirt, and she's on her way to her first day as Assistant to the Private Secretary of the Prime

Minister of Australia. Yep, there I was in the land of Oz all right, but my tornado of chance had somehow managed to hurl me far enough along the yellow brick road to land right inside the Wizard's castle in one fell swoop—right over that dreaded typing pool and into the Prime Minister's office, the private chambers of the big Wiz himself.

This was definitely an amazing opportunity and a fast-tracked and very steep learning curve for any teenager. And for me it was a Magical first step into adult life. Somehow, the combination of my own will and sheer serendipity had thrown me right smack in the middle of Australian and world politics where some incredible people were right there making history.

I knew I was in the middle of a special and amazing experience—I couldn't help but know—and I carefully savoured everything I was seeing and feeling around me. Being in those rooms and echoey halls of the old Parliament House in Canberra, especially during those tumultuous first few months, brushing past visiting Heads of State in the hallways, talking to the PM on the phone, sitting in his office taking down a letter, being among the Hansard writers—

was all Magic and I loved it for as long as it lasted.

I had many minor yet momentous moments in that time, like taking a cup of tea to Sir Arthur Caldwell, one of the founders of Australia's Labor Party, as he sat in his musty old office looking just like a character from a Charles Dickens novel. A big, ageing man hunched over his large antique desk, surrounded by hundreds of dusty books and yellowing piles of papers.

I met them all, Ministers, members of the House of Reps, Senators, and many of the past and future Prime Ministers—including Bob Hawke, and Sir Malcolm Fraser, before he informed a future Australia that 'life wasn't meant to be easy'. And of course the biggest ol' Wiz of all, Gough Whitlam,

in his pre-Prime Minister days—right before he became a national treasure and icon.

Yep, interesting stuff indeed and a real eye-opener, like the time my first boss, Sir John Gorton, and everyone in his office were suddenly and unceremoniously ousted by his own party—all except little ol' me. Amazingly, I was the only one in the PM's office who was asked to stay, and I was then promoted and went on to work for the incoming Prime Minister, Sir William McMahon.

And so what happened to this promising career in politics? Well, eight months and two Prime Ministers later, just as I was finally getting the hang of manoeuvring the front steps of Parliament House in my 12-inch platform shoes, I unexpectedly won a teen Model of the Year competition, which I'd entered as a bit of a lark, and a picture of me wearing leather hotpants was splashed over the front pages of a national newspaper, along with the headline: 'Look who's working in the Prime Minister's office!'

Well, not too surprisingly, the powers that be over at Parliament House were not too impressed by my media debut. And they seemed quite relieved when I admitted that I had been offered a contract with well-known modelling agency Vivien's Management and I'd been considering leaving Parliament House and moving up to Sydney. Well, Sir William's people really couldn't do enough to help speed me on my way to pursue this alternative career. And they agreed with me wholeheartedly that I should take up this wonderful opportunity straight away—immediately, pronto—and move far away from Canberra, our nation's capital and the Prime Minister's office, as soon as possible.

'Why, I reckon you'll soon be travelling abroad, away from Australia, far, far, far away,' one of them said rather hopefully. The mind boggles as to what would have happened if they had ever found out about my witchy nature.

And so my exciting time in politics and the Castle of Oz came to an abrupt end. But I wasn't too upset—I knew there were many other adventures ahead and, let's face it, once you've seen the real goings-on at the round table of the 'inner sanctum', when you've already met the Ol' Wiz and his Castle Favourites, and seen the storytellers spinning their clever tales and building their glittery myths and legends for the people, what do you do and where do you go from there?

Well, for me there was to be only one choice: it was time for me to look for some real Magic.

It was time for me to go back down the other side of the yellow brick road and find a real Wizard—and perhaps, on the way, learn how to be a Real Witch.

A Model Witchling

I arrived in Sydney in the swinging 70s. The modelling agency had found me a small, two-roomed terrace in the inner city, just down the end of Liverpool Street and within walking distance of the hippest shops, cafes and clubs. I shared the house with another young model who had just arrived from the country and, girls being girls, neither of us wasted any time jumping headlong into big-city living and all the fun and trouble we could find.

Despite quite a few days of missed appointments and way too many late-night parties, I actually started being booked for some great assignments and eventually was photographed for the covers and fashion pages of magazines like *Dolly*, *Cleo* and *Cosmopolitan*, and began appearing on the catwalks and in television commercials for anything from ice-cream to sports cars.

Here I was again, hurtling along another fast learning-curve and having some amazing experiences. I had just turned 16 and was now working with some of the best photographers, magazines and advertising agencies around, as well as socialising with a flamboyant bunch of creative, talented and highly strung fashion folk.

Of course I enjoyed the excitement and glamour of it all. Like a lot of teenage girls, I had dreamt of working as a fashion model since I was a little kid, and here I was in the big city living out one of my major dreams.

But a year or so on, I started seeing a lot of the shallowness behind the glamour, as well experiencing the inevitable down-side of being valued for just my physical appearance. Modelling can be creatively satisfying and great fun, but your success depends on maintaining an unreal image of beauty and a certain lifestyle that I began to resent.

I managed to pull it off for a while, until I started to get the distinct

impression that I was walking through a kind of a fantasy land full of plastic talking dolls. I was confused and disturbed by how unsatisfying my life was quickly becoming. But at the same time I didn't want to just turn my back on the more artistic and creative aspects of my work, which I still really enjoyed.

I was also very aware that these great jobs and opportunities wouldn't last forever, and I pushed myself to keep going.

But I felt like stranger in a strange land, a square peg in a round hole, and I sensed that another big life change was on the cards. This one, however, was more of an inner, spiritual change, and one that would eventually help me to make sense of who I was and how I was going to fit into a world that was starting to feel bizarre and more and more remote.

Looking back, I think I was driven by the natural instincts of spiritual survival.

I was also at one of those major crossroads in a young person's life where I needed to find my true path and understand all the different facets and choices of who and what I could become as an adult.

The Magic
is there inside you,
just waiting to be discovered.
You have the power
to make it happen.

The Inner Witch Blossoms

That was around the time that I started looking further into my Celtic heritage and the inner lore of witchcraft and took my first conscious steps to find a mentor. As well as exploring my own Magical background, I began a complete frenzy of mystical study: I learnt about astrology, the tarot and the power of crystals; practised throwing the I Ching; and I looked into yoga, meditation and the spiritual teachings of Eastern philosophies, including Buddhism and Hinduism.

I was also passionately drawn to discover and experience other cultures and writers like Kahlil Gibran, Carlos Castanada and the many other inspirational authors who were popular at that time. Of course, there were thousands of other people who, just like me, were beginning to look at alternatives to the mainstream religions and philosophies.

The 1970s were definitely a time of spiritual action and awakening for many people. More and more valuable ancient knowledge was becoming publicly available on the various philosophies and more and more spiritual teachers and 'gurus' began to miraculously appear around the world as their students simultaneously started searching around and gravitating towards them.

Because I was also on a mission to find my own Magical path I was always open to meeting a spiritual master, and was fortunate enough to meet a couple of the internationally respected gurus of the time. But, despite respecting their traditions and teachings, I still felt that somewhere out there was the right teacher for me.

At that time, during the 1960s and 1970s, there was very limited public information and few books available about the Craft, and in Australia the practice of witchcraft was not only still grossly misunderstood, but actually illegal (the Witchcraft Act was finally repealed as late as 1971). So the only

real hope for a Magical seeker to learn anything worthwhile was if you were lucky enough to stumble across one of the very few and hidden covens.

There's an old saying:
'When the student is ready, the master will appear'.

Somehow, in the middle of all this universal cosmic soup, I was introduced to mine through a good friend, a lovely young guy called David.

David was an artist. He rode a motorbike, he was handsome in a sleepy kind of way and lived like a rebellious rascal. Just my kind of man. He was also a very spiritual young guy, and wise before his time in many ways. David often spoke about a very interesting man, a parapsychologist and mystic who'd been helping out a mutual friend of ours who was going through some serious personal and business problems.

To cut a long story short, our friend, Jim, was a young entrepreneur who had unfortunately not only lost his savings and reputation in a failed business venture, but was also being hounded by various TV crews and news reporters who were staking out his home and shoving cameras and microphones in his face at every opportunity. With the whole 'hard copy' media frenzy, right on top of losing everything, he was becoming quite desperate and almost suicidal. As a last resort, he sought some spiritual advice to help find some answers and perhaps a way out of the mess he was in.

That spiritual adviser happened to be Edgar Pielke, one of Australia's best known and respected witches of the 1970s, and the man whom I was to later know by his Craft name 'Fenris, the Master Druid'. I was completely enthralled as I heard how the Druid Master had advised Jim to organise a television interview with a current affairs program. Apparently, he had also advised that the interview be held not in a studio, but outdoors in a tree-

filled location. Just as the interview began, the Druid Master concealed himself behind a grove of trees where, undetected by the TV crews, he could direct his powerful energy towards Jim and the reporter interviewing him. Like a scene from the legends of King Arthur, this modern-day wizard and Master of Magic performed an ancient rite of protection and empowerment, and lo and behold, Jim answered all the questions the reporter fired at him with honesty and dignity.

It proved to be the turning point in the whole debacle and after that, Jim's reputation was delicately put back together again. What impressed me the most was that before he went into that interview, the Druid Master had shown Jim how to balance his perspective on everything. He told him to meditate on the fact that his current problems were in fact a special gift that had brought his soul back to its rightful path, and, instead of lamenting over losing everything, he should actually be celebrating a new beginning. Jim had gone into that meeting filled with his own sense of power. He had been shown how to overcome his feelings of loss and despair, and how to reach a point of calm confidence.

That story really fascinated and amazed me. I had already studied some yoga and the meditation techniques of the various Asian-based philosophies, and had read about the possibility of reaching a true state of peace. I sensed that there were many truths among all of these teachings but, other than just as a way of relaxing and calming the mind and body, I had never fully understood the significance of meditation or the state of just 'being'. I was not even sure if it was really possible to attain it.

My hair stood up on end when I got a real glimpse of what all of this could mean, and I suddenly understood that the Druid Master had actually shown Jim how to reach a balanced *non*-state of being. And then he had taken the technique one step further, and had focused that energy into very powerful Magic. He had cast a spell and I knew I had to meet this masterful Witch.

Meeting the Druid Master

It was 1975, chamois bikinis and crocheted anything were all the rage, the current Prime Minister, Gough Whitlam, had been dismissed from the Castle of Oz, and I was on my way to meet a Master Wizard.

I hopped onto the back of David's motorbike, and felt my stomach churn with anticipation. We were going to a party at Jim's beautiful waterfront property in Vaucluse, to celebrate a housewarming and a new beginning.

The Druid Master was also going to be at the party with his coven, and even though I was dying to meet him, I was unbelievably nervous. My heart was beating a million times a minute.

Will he see inside my soul? What if he doesn't like what he sees?

I was petrified at the prospect of someone being able to see inside my head or possibly knowing who I was (even before I did), and yet at the same time I was utterly compelled to find out.

David freewheeled down Jim's winding driveway in neutral and parked next to a shiny collection of imported cars; apparently Jim had bounced back very well from the brink of disaster. Jim's girlfriend Sonia waved to us from the open door and we were soon inside, in the middle of a large crowd, smiling a little stiffly at people we didn't know very well. With a glass of red wine in hand we offered some awkward small talk while both nervously looking sideways for any sign of the Druid Master.

We'd arrived late, so the party had been going on for quite a while and there was a chance he'd already left, so I started to just relax and enjoy myself a little more. Eventually, I wandered over to the terrace for a breath of fresh air. That's when I saw Jim through the balcony window, smiling and waving at me to come over.

As I stepped towards him onto the terrace, a sudden, massive wave of energy travelled up from my feet to the top of my head, and Jim caught my arm just before I toppled over head first. Embarrassed, I straightened myself up, turned, and looked straight into the eyes of a Lord of Light.

You know those times in your life when you experience a true epiphany?

A timeless moment when you realise with all certainty that you are experiencing something of great meaning and significance? That's how I felt in that instant. I was no longer scared or nervous about revealing who I was to anyone. I felt entirely relaxed, but at the same time empowered with the wonder of seeing my own spirit reflected through this energy source. Time seemed to grind into slow motion. It was like being in the eye of a storm, that small space where everything is still in the middle of chaos. I also sensed a feeling of déjà vu, a recognition that I had experienced this type of energy before—during a near-death experience I'd had in the middle of the Nullarbor Plain.

I had been travelling with a friend on a 3,000 kilometre trip through the remote interior of Australia. I was having a nap in the back of our car as we drove along the then untarred, sunbaked dirt road that was the Simpson Highway. Suddenly, without warning, the car hit a huge pothole in the road at 100 kilometres per hour. As the car rolled over five or six times, I was mentally preparing myself for death. I was certain that I was looking at my last few seconds of life on Earth.

But, somehow, amongst all the shattering glass and crushing metal, I felt myself surrounded by what I can only describe as some type of 'caring energy'. It gently pushed me through a hole in the back window, and as I was being catapulted through the air, time seemed to slow right down. I remember seeing nothing but an endless and magnificent light which spoke to me. It said: 'Relax, Deborah, it's not your time yet, everything is going to be all right.'

I then had time to enjoy the sensation of soaring like a bird through the air—until I landed like a sack of potatoes on the rock-hard desert floor at least 10 metres away from the crumpled car, flat on my back, with the breath completely knocked out of me. But, incredibly, I was able to stand up right then with nothing to show for it but a pair of ripped jeans. I had no broken bones, in fact I walked way from the completely squashed car without a scratch. A couple of hours later, we were sipping a cup of hot tea with a young Aboriginal couple who had found us wandering dazed in the middle of Never Never Land and had brought us back to their camp.

I had reflected on that life and death experience many times over, and now here I was on a balcony in Sydney, looking straight into that same boundless Universe. And again I was aware of that same shifting of time, the endless well of incredible light and energy, and the aroma of smouldering ashes.

When my vision cleared and I could start to make out physical shapes again, there was a grey-haired man aged around 50 or so standing right in front of me. He looked like a Native American Indian, with a slightly hooked nose, carved cheekbones and long, flowing hair. A split second later, he turned slightly and at a different angle reflected yet another face—this one entirely Nordic, like a young Viking soldier. An instant later and at another angle, an old Sorcerer, with piercing light blue eyes and pale skin appeared.

His face kept morphing between these three images, as if they were three facets of one crystal. But then the face of the Old Sorcerer remained and the words 'Yes, this is Fenris' appeared in my mind.

He was wearing a simple long white caftan, but around his neck was a very ornate and magnificently carved silver pendant. It was fashioned in the shape of a circle and magenta stones and rubies encrusted its centre. It was as if it had been styled by an ancient silversmith, with a mixture of Celtic and Nordic designs, and coiled, swirling fronds spraying outwards like metallic ferns or the rays of a silver sun.

Next to him stood an exotic, raven-haired young woman who also wore a flowing white dress. There were others, too, including a rather gothic couple who sat nearby softly strumming their Spanish-style guitars and singing. But I couldn't focus on anyone else; it was all I could do to stop from falling into the piercing blue eyes of the Druid Master.

'Ah Deborah you're finally here,' he said. 'We've been waiting for you.'

I stammered something like, 'We had to stop for petrol,' but I knew that was not what he meant. I knew with every thread and cell of my being that he was talking to my soul.

I was in the middle of an eternal moment, I was meeting a very old friend, and I was Home.

DREAM VISION, 1973
Are we still in the present, or is this the future of the past? These are the most incredible blue eyes I have ever seen, there's a faint scent of sage and now he's beside me again and we've been walking for days through the Nullarbor Desert. We stop to drink from a small billabong the colour of sapphires and burnt cinnamon.

Behind the Secret Veil

And speaking of mind body and spirit connection, I really got the giggles the other day when I read a letter from someone who wanted to know what kind of Magical clothes our coven members wore. Immediately this spirited conversation between the Druid Master and me, during one of my first skyclad meetings, came back to mind. I thought I might share it with you so you can enjoy the experience of being 'behind the secret veil' at a witches' gathering.

'Banishing inhibitions? I don't have any inhibitions—but I could never sit naked in front of a whole lot of other people.'
'Oh really, how come?'
'Because I don't think that sex or nudity has anything to do with spirituality or metaphysics.'
'Who said anything about sex?'
'Well that's what usually happens when someone takes off their clothes.'
'Oh, every time? Like at the beach, or when you're taking a shower?'
'Well, of course not every time, but in normal circumstances to be naked in front of other people...I mean in normal society, everyone knows...Umm well that's what can or usually does happen.'
'Oh I see, in normal society. And where are you now?'
'I'm in a house, your house, sitting in a living room, talking with a few other people.'
'Look around, do you know where you are exactly?'

'Yes, I'm in a witch's coven.'
'And why are you here?'
'I'm here to learn.'

A heartbeat later, the penny drops and so do all my clothes as I silently disrobe and sit comfortably naked on a red velvet cushion feeling as joyous and free as a bird in the sky.
And now do you know where you are?'
'Yes I know exactly where I am.'
'And who are you?'
'I'm Deborah,'
And what are you?'
'I'm a woman and I'm a witch'
— Skyclad meeting, The Circle of Light, 1975

Now for those who might not at first get the gist of the above conversation, it is that although some witches prefer to work in special Magical robes, some witches and covens disrobe and have 'skyclad' meetings. Performing rituals naked really has nothing to do with sex orgies or titillation—it has got to do with freedom and harmony and letting go of the boundaries of society's shame and guilt about your beautiful God/dess-given body. It has to do with reconnecting with your personal sacred temple, your own miraculous body which enables you to experience all facets of life and physicality in this dimension.

For me personally, the freeing up of my own inhibitions and understanding the mind/body/spirit connection had practical benefits by enhancing my self confidence as an actress and singer. This directly led to the incredible honour of being asked to sit for a portrait by the famous artist Charles Billich—who was mystically inspired to portray me as a Magical 'triple goddess', in a beautiful life-sized oil painting that was later auctioned in aid of a Children's Hospital telethon and now graces almost an entire wall of one of Australia's largest private art galleries.

When the student is ready, the master will appear

Hex In The City

Many Full Moons after those first ventures of mine into the big wide world, I had moved to New York to study music and theatre at the famous Stella Adler school and to sing in the smoky jazz cafes of Manhattan. It was many years since I had first met the Druid Master and I had continued my Magical studies while juggling a busy career as an actress and singer/songwriter throughout the 1970s and '80s.

From 1975 onwards I had lived in the family environment of a coven house. During that time and just a few years after my witchy initiation, I made my debut as an actress on Australian television. I played the now legendary role of the nubile and rather sexy Miss Hemmingway on *No. 96* (I never do anything by halves!). After that I had numerous roles on TV shows such as *The Young Doctors*, *Kingswood Country*, *Catch Us If You Can*, *Bellamy*, *Best of Friends* and *Power and the Passion*.

Eventually, I moved into my own home in the mid-1980s and travelled overseas for work assignments such as writing music for the Olympic ice-skaters Torvill and Dean, fulfilling recording contracts and show tours throughout Germany and Europe and, in the '90s, singing assignments in New York jazz clubs including Maxims, Blue Note and the Supper Club. And all that time I remained a practising witch and a member of the Edgar/Fenris circle.

Like all students, I developed my own style and techniques.

They will always incorporate my original training, but now my own feminine Goddess energies, individual perceptions and experiences filter through and permeate my Magic.

My spiritual teacher Edgar's genetic background (Edgar Pielke—Fenris, the Druid Master) was German and Celtic, and his Magical traditions and

Occult knowledge were from a long history of family lore and training that also reflected his ancestry. He had become a Master Witch and what is known in the Craft as an 'Ipsissimus' through a series of family initiations followed by life-altering experiences where fate put him through a number of 'vision quests' and extreme tests of courage and will.

One of them was when he was around 16 and he was conscripted into the German army. He was taught to drive a panzer tank and sent out to the Russian Front towards the end of World War II. He was captured by the Russians and sent to a Siberian concentration camp where he remained for a terrible few years. It was during this hard vigil of loneliness, starvation, extreme cold and inhuman conditions that he first travelled 'over the abyss' and only his early Occult training and natural ability helped guide him through and saved his life. A great benefit from his time there was his discovery of his own unbreakable sense of purpose and his True Will to be a master of the Ancient Mysteries.

During my early years in the coven, Edgar appeared on many current-affairs programs and did frequent television and radio interviews. He spoke about witchcraft on discussion panels with mainstream and conservative religious leaders.

During his life, Edgar was a groundbreaker in a lot of ways.

He was one of the first male witches and coven leaders in Australia to 'come out' in the media after the anti-witchcraft laws were repealed in 1971. (The Kings Cross artist Rosaleen Norton was the first female witch to previously 'come out' to the Aussie media. Rosaleen had visited Edgar's

Darlinghurst-based coven in the late 1960s and early '70s to discuss the rising interest in and portrayal of the Craft in the media.)

We often had journalists come to our house to interview Edgar for newspaper stories and books (including Craft historian Nevill Drury, author of many excellent books, including *Other Temples, Other Gods*, where he refers to Edgar as one of Australia's best-known witches of the time).

On the whole, many of the Australian journalists considered Edgar to be one of the most adept spokespersons on the Occult and respected his unique opinions and communication skills highly. He was dedicated to his life mission as a teacher, and was determined to dispel the negative myths and misconceptions about the Craft. I gained a lot of valuable insights from those times. We would often accompany him when he was being interviewed by any of a long list of well-known journalists, including Mike Willesee, Clive Hale, Derryn Hinch, Caroline Jones, Mike Walsh and Mike Minnehan.

Many international personalities of the day were intrigued too. Irish showman Dave Allen, the famous Doctor Who, and even the legendary Benny Hill—whom I worked with in a TV special—were fascinated by our coven (Benny especially, who despite his fame as a slapstick comedian, was actually a deeply serious and intelligent man).

Our witches' circle also managed to develop quite a good relationship with the media over the years, and reporters usually respected coven members' right to privacy and anonymity whenever they requested it. Even when my photo was inevitably splashed over the front page of the newspapers with the headline: 'Leading actress admits she's a witch,' the story on the inside pages was actually quite fair and balanced.

It was just a matter of time before my 'secret double life' as a witch was made

233

public in the late 1970s. I had already become well-known as a television personality, and when I started being interviewed at the coven house by journalists about my acting and singing career, it must have been pretty obvious to even the most unobservant visitors that there was a certain air of 'mystery' (to put it mildly) around our house.

I've never shied away from telling people what spiritual path I follow, but only if they specifically ask me. I've never been ashamed or embarrassed by the necessary explanations, no matter how tricky it was to speak openly about witchcraft way back in those more conventional days, when 'practising witch' was definitely not something most people put on their résumé.

Edgar passed on to his next phase of life in the early 1990s (though he still continues to visit me in my dreams and visions, just as he has done for aeons) and throughout all these years I have applied his teachings, along with my own Magical inspirations, to my creative work, music, relationships and life in the 'real' world.

Most of the remaining members of our coven are now living in different parts of the world. We'd all spent many years going through big changes, ups and downs, comings and goings, losses and triumphs, but the inner core always remained close and the coven 'flame' is still burning brightly.

Athena Starwoman and I met in the late 1970s when she first came to meet Edgar, and even though she didn't live in the coven house, she was a frequent visitor and a great student of Magic. She and I soon became close friends and while Athena's work as a world-famous astrologer took her to places far and wide, we always considered each other sisters in spirit and close allies in helping to bring the mystical and Magical back to the modern world.

There we were back then, still following the gypsy life and living on the other side of the planet in New York City. I had managed to find a great loft apartment in the West Village and we'd spend any spare moment going to SoHo or the East Village of Manhattan searching out all of the hidden-

away and gloriously bohemian witchy shops. We'd be on the lookout for old grimoires and Magical curios and knick-knacks (as well as the occasional cute boy witch or two).

We had lots of hysterically funny experiences in the Big Apple, like the time we were wondering where to find an old-fashioned alchemy shop to stock up on some spell ingredients, and Athena suddenly exclaimed, 'Hey, this is New York, just look in the Yellow Pages under "Occult"'. So, just like in an episode of *Bewitched*, we flipped through the Yellow Pages and there it was—a fabulous advertisement saying: 'Fresh supplies of dragon's tail and hexing powder, 20 per cent off graveyard dust'. When I called the shop's number a very sweet voice answered with 'Enchantment Incorporated, can I help you?'

In fact, it was during those years that Athena and I started writing *How To Turn Your Ex-Boyfriend Into a Toad*, after we'd searched around and realised that there were very few decipherable books on spellcasting, and even fewer that included fun and humour from the perspective of a modern city witch.

We also loved to spend time reminiscing and giggling about the early coven days in the 1970s when unsuspecting visitors would nervously knock at the door of the grand old Art Deco coven house in Sydney, to be greeted by the baying of the Hounds of the Baskervilles (really just our arthritic old German shepherd and various rescued pound dogs barking in unison).

Most visitors would almost faint on the spot as the door would slowly creak open and one or other of the girls of the house would be standing there, resplendent with flowing hair, witchy jewellery and diaphanous gown. I'll never forget the look on the face of a particular photographer who had been sent over by a TV station to take some pictures of me for a magazine. As soon as he knocked on the door, all six of our dogs rushed barking like crazy into the front hall and scared the life out of him. He admitted to me later that when I opened the door in my long white dress, calmly holding

all the 'hounds of Hell' back with one hand and carrying Lucy, our black shingleback lizard in the other, he almost dropped his camera and made a run for it.

The Addams Family had nothing on us!

Of course, if a visitor was lucky enough to be invited home to meet our 'family', the *pièce de résistance* would be when they were ushered into our Metaphysic Room (much like an old-style drawing room), and they'd see our witch's altar draped in wine-red velvet, with a giant, ornately carved mirror hanging overhead, complete with ancient Magical symbols and two engraved candelabra sitting on either side of a pair of matching skulls. At this point they would either turn around and hightail it out the front door in terror, or they would immediately relax and settle in to spend a great evening philosophising with the Druid Master and the rest of the coven, drinking aged port from our best set of chalice cups, or playing chess and listening to the songs and music that were usually being performed by someone in the house, until the early hours of the morning.

But not everyone agreed with my spiritual choice, especially back in the 1970s and '80s.

There was still quite a lot of misunderstanding about and even fear of covens and witches, and some people were downright insulting and tried to do their best to bring me 'back to my senses'. Despite these people's misgivings and sometimes laughable perceptions of what witches do, however, I just kept on rediscovering this ancient path of harmony and self-knowledge. Sure, socialising and explaining my private life to work colleagues and the media has been very tricky sometimes. And very few boyfriends felt comfortable around my mentor in those early days, either— many mistakenly believed they were competing for my affection. But, nevertheless, I hung in there, and reaped the benefits of this way of life and of having such a wonderful spiritual guide.

I always felt that our coven house was quite a sacred environment, similar in many ways to a Buddhist temple or an ancient school of philosophy and alchemy. As soon as you walked in the door, you felt the energy shift and the communal focus come into play. Spells, rituals and any ceremonial Magic were only taught after willingness and readiness to accept and understand the seemingly mundane and simple day-to-day chores of growing up. You would often hear dialogues that went like:

> *'Clean the Metaphysic Room, Deborah.'*
> *'But it wasn't me who made the mess!'*
> *'Clean the Metaphysic Room, Deborah.'*
> *'But how come I've got to do it again?'*
> *'Because you need to clean it again.'*

There was plenty of spiritual discipline throughout my early training, but there was also a great deal of humour, creativity, music and lots of love—along with all the normal personality clashes and arguments you'd expect in a group of strong-minded people. And there was the loud foot-stomping of neophytes in the face of reflected truth.

The various members of our coven had a wide variety of ambitions and professions, including law, science and medicine, and we still needed to go out each day and actually apply these spiritual lessons and 'practical Magic' in our jobs. We went on living with outside society as we earned our livings, built our careers, socialised and carried on our everyday lives as people in a large, modern city, in perfect balance with what we were simultaneously coming to understand in the coven.

I was and have always been an urban witch, although I do adore the Magic of the countryside and the more natural environments, and it has been a constant challenge to apply certain country folk traditions and old-style aspects of the Craft to city living, that's for sure. Many times I've been tempted to go and live in a rainforest or live full-time in the beautiful

Australian bush growing herbs. But I figure if your work is in the city, you have to learn to adapt.

You actually need to go to the core of the meaning of Magic practice, so you can learn to be flexible and to be able to take it on the road with you anywhere.

This approach has worked well for me over the years. Apart from working in the performing arts in Australia, my television roles and singing career have taken me to just about every country on the planet. And wherever I go, I continue to practice my craft, in New York, Los Angeles, London, Munich, Paris, Singapore and Tokyo. Because once you've learnt how to tap into the source of real Magic, once you've accessed that Universal power and touched the face of your own eternal and Magical spirit—there's no looking back. It changes you forever. You become a self-contained and mobile Magic-maker and no matter what emotional or physical circumstances you're in, you can apply that knowledge, connect with your higher self and use any of the tried and true techniques to weave your spells and charms wherever and whenever you want to.

Reference Books and Recommended Reading

William Bottrell, *Cornish Witches and Cunning Men*, Oakmagic Publications, Cornwall.

Raymond Buckland, *Buckland's Complete Book of Witchcraft*, Llewellyn Publications, St Paul, Minnesota, 1986.

Pauline and Dan Campanelli, *Ancient Ways: Reclaiming Pagan Traditions*, Llewellyn Publications, St Paul, Minnesota, 1991.

Paul Carus, *The Teachings of Buddha*, St Martins Press, New York, 1998.

Paul F. Case, *The Tarot: Key to the Wisdom of the Ages*, BOTA, Los Angeles, 1990.

Deepak Chopra, *How to Know God*, Harmony Books (Random House), New York, 2000.

Kerr Cuhulain, *Wiccan Warrior: Walking a Spiritual Path in a Sometimes Hostile World*, Llewellyn Worldwide, St Paul, Minnesota, 2000.

Dr John F. Demartini, *Count Your Blessings: The Healing Power of Gratitude and Love*, Element Books, Massachusetts, 1997.

Nevill Drury, *Everyday Magic: Empowering Our Lives Through the Magical Wisdom Traditions*, Simon and Schuster, Sydney, 2001.

Nevill Drury, *The History of Magic in the Modern Age: A Quest for Personal Transformation*, Simon & Schuster, Sydney, 2000.

Dion Fortune, *The Esoteric Orders and Their Work*, Aquarian Press, London, 1987.

Timothy Freke and Peter Gandy, *The Hermetica: The Lost Wisdom of the Pharaohs*, Judy Piatkus Publishers, London, 1997.

Rene-Maurice Gattefosse, *Gattefosse's Aromatherapy* (English translation by Robert B. Tisserand), C.W. Daniel Co. Ltd., Saffron Walden, Essex, 1993.

Raven Grimassi, *Wiccan Magick: Inner Teachings of the Craft*, Llewellyn Publications, St Paul, Minnesota, 1998.

Rosemary Ellen Guiley, *The Encyclopedia of Witches and Witchcraft*, Checkmark Books, New York, 1999.

Frank Herbert, *Dune* (first published in 1965), Ace Books, New York, 1999.

Ronald Hutton, *The Triumph of the Moon: A History of Modern Pagan Witchcraft*, Oxford University Press, New York, 1999.

John King, *The Modern Numerology: A Practical Guide to the Meaning and Influence of Numbers*, Blandford Publishers, London, 1996.

Julia Lawless, *The Illustrated History of Essential Oils*, Element Books Inc., Rockport, Massachusetts, 1997.

Phoenix McFarland, *The Complete Book of Magical Names*, Llewellyn Publications, St Paul, Minnesota, 1996.

Louis MacNeice, *Astrology*, Aldus Books, London, and Doubleday, New York, 1964.

Jean Markale, *The Druids: Celtic Priests of Nature* (English translation by Jon Graham), Inner Traditions International, Rochester, Vermont, 1999.

John O'Donohue, *Anam Cara: Spiritual Wisdom from the Celtic World*, Bantam Press, London, 1997.

David Sheinkin, *Path of the Kabbalah*, Paragon House, New York, 1986.

Starhawk, *The Spiral Dance: A Rebirth of the Ancient Tradition of the Great Goddess*, HarperSanFrancisco, California, 1999.

Athena Starwoman, *Zodiac: Your Astrology Guide to the New Millennium*, HarperCollins, Sydney, 2000.

Marion Weinstein, *Positive Magic: Occult Self-Help*, Earth Magic Productions, Eugene, Oregon, 1997.

Spellfinder
Find a spell, charm or magical cure at a glance

For information on Deborah's catalogue or potions, please write to:
PO Box 229, Woollahra NSW 2025 Australia
Website: www.deborahgraymagic.com
e-mail: info@deborahgray.com